ROUNDTABLE ON TECHNICAL LEADERSHIP

A SHAPE Forum Dialogue

Also Available from Dorset House Publishing

Amplifying Your Effectiveness: Collected Essays
edited by Gerald M. Weinberg, James Bach, and Naomi Karten
ISBN: 0-932633-47-1 Copyright ©2000 160 pages, softcover

Exploring Requirements: Quality Before Design
by Donald C. Gause and Gerald M. Weinberg
ISBN: 0-932633-13-7 Copyright ©1989 320 pages, hardcover

An Introduction to General Systems Thinking: Silver Anniversary Edition
by Gerald M. Weinberg
ISBN: 0-932633-49-8 Copyright ©2001 304 pages, softcover

More Secrets of Consulting: The Consultant's Tool Kit
by Gerald M. Weinberg
ISBN: 0-932633-52-8 Copyright ©2002 216 pages, softcover

Peopleware: Productive Projects and Teams, 2nd ed.
by Tom DeMarco and Timothy Lister
ISBN: 0-932633-43-9 Copyright ©1999 264 pages, softcover

Project Retrospectives: A Handbook for Team Reviews
by Norman L. Kerth foreword by Gerald M. Weinberg
ISBN: 0-932633-44-7 Copyright ©2001 288 pages, softcover

The Psychology of Computer Programming: Silver Anniversary Edition
by Gerald M. Weinberg
ISBN: 0-932633-42-0 Copyright ©1998 360 pages, softcover

Roundtable on Project Management: A SHAPE Forum Dialogue
edited by James Bullock, Gerald M. Weinberg, and Marie Benesh
ISBN: 0-932633-48-X Copyright ©2001 200 pages, softcover

The Secrets of Consulting: A Guide to Giving and Getting Advice Successfully
by Gerald M. Weinberg foreword by Virginia Satir
ISBN: 0-932633-01-3 Copyright ©1985 248 pages, softcover

An Independent Publisher of Books on
Systems and Software Development and Management. Since 1984.

- Contact us for prices, shipping options, availability, and more.
- Sign up for *DHQ: The Dorset House Quarterly* in print or PDF.
- Send e-mail to subscribe to *e-DHQ,* our e-mail newsletter.
- Visit Dorsethouse.com for excerpts, reviews, downloads, and more.

DORSET HOUSE PUBLISHING
353 West 12th Street New York, NY 10014 USA
1-800-DH-BOOKS 1-800-342-6657
212-620-4053 fax: 212-727-1044
info@dorsethouse.com www.dorsethouse.com

ROUNDTABLE ON TECHNICAL LEADERSHIP

A SHAPE Forum Dialogue

edited by Gerald M. Weinberg,
Marie Benesh,
and James Bullock,

DORSET HOUSE PUBLISHING
353 WEST 12TH STREET
NEW YORK, NEW YORK 10014

Library of Congress Cataloging-in-Publication Data

Roundtable on technical leadership : a SHAPE forum dialogue / edited by Gerald M. Weinberg, Marie Benesh, and James Bullock.
p. cm.
Includes bibliographical references and index.
ISBN 0-932633-51-X
1. Computer software--Development--Management. I. Weinberg, Gerald M. II. Benesh, Marie. III. Bullock, James.

QA76.76.D47 R68 2002
005.1'068--dc21

2002019302

Cover Design: David W. McClintock
Interior Illustrations: Rich Terdoslavich

Distributed in the English language in Singapore, the Philippines, and Southeast Asia by Alkem Company (S) Pte. Ltd., Singapore; in the English language in India, Bangladesh, Sri Lanka, Nepal, and Mauritius by Prism Books Pvt., Ltd., Bangalore, India; and in the English language in Japan by Toppan Co., Ltd., Tokyo, Japan.

Printed in the United States of America

Library of Congress Catalog Number: 2002019302

ISBN: 0-932633-51-X 12 11 10 9 8 7 6 5 4 3 2 1

Contents

CONTRIBUTORS

JIM BATTERSON
Jim Batterson is an independent consultant living in Richmond, Virginia. He is currently interested in the craft of storytelling, and in particular, positive and uplifting stories from the annals of the cubicle farm that so many of us in the technical world call our home away from home.

MARIE BENESH
Marie is principal of Benesh & Associates, an IT management consulting firm. With her wide range of experience in IT management, Marie advises clients on the issues that arise in managing human resources, strategy development and implementation, organization design, team development, and large-scale project definition and management. Marie combines a strong background in technology and enterprise architecture with a natural talent for implementing the governance and people structures that make an organizational architecture effective.

Readers may contact the contributors through Dorset House Publishing at info@dorsethouse.com.

Marie has implemented leading practices in software engineering for organizations, and understands the management of application development organizations. She has a wealth of experience in project assessment and consulting in PeopleSoft, an ERP-based system. She has utilized her skills in Program Management, Infrastructure Implementation and Management, Release Management, IT/User Test Planning, and Implementation within the university and corporate arenas. Her clientele include major universities and Fortune 500 corporations.

She focuses much of her consulting on the development of IT leadership skills through individual coaching and mentoring, performance-based review and development processes, and team design and management. Marie participates actively in groups that are focused on uncovering leading practices in IT management and in providing experiential learning opportunities for leaders.

JAMES BULLOCK

In his more than eighteen years of building systems, from lab automation and high-volume embedded controls to enterprise data warehousing and ERP deployments, James Bullock has been everything from a coding "grunt" to a high-priced consultant. Some of his embedded controls are still deployed, and a data warehouse he architected six years ago is still in use, among other apparent successes. More important to James is the contact he maintains with some folks from previous projects—people who not only built something good, but enjoyed doing it.

Over time, James has become more interested in how we go about building systems than in the systems themselves. Jerry Weinberg's SHAPE forum allows him to explore that.

PAT FERDINANDI **www.SBDi-consulting.com**

Pat is the president of Strategic Business Decisions, a consulting company specializing in requirements engineering, project management, and process improvement. Pat's latest contribution is the introduction of a Requirements Pattern (including Anti-Patterns) that assists in capturing a fuller requirements set for any type of project. The Requirements Pattern is currently being used by Fortune 500 companies and will be discussed in her forthcoming book: *A Requirements Pattern: Succeeding in an Internet Economy.*

As a diversion from the hectic pace of Wall Street, Pat—with the help of her two-and-a-half-year-old Solomon Island Eclectus, Scarlet—developed a *Companion Parrot Care Guide* as a donation to the Oasis Sanctuary Foundation (www.theoasis.org). This thirty-six-page booklet eases the transfer involved in temporary vacations and provides instructions for permanent care by fully describing the specific needs of your parrot.

FRITZ

Fritz has facilitated the technical work of system administrators by developing software tools; now he's learning to facilitate the human work of tool developers.

PHIL FUHRER

Phil Fuhrer is a systems architect at VoiceCue Technologies, which provides voice recognition, response, real-time billing, and provisioning systems for wireless networks. Previously, with thirty years of experience at Bell Laboratories, Phil was responsible for architecture, reliability, performance, network management, and requirements for telephone switching and other systems. His career spans analog and digital networks, and he is looking forward to implementing wireless broadband services. He specializes in reviews, human development, and team effectiveness.

JESSE M. GORDON

Jesse M. Gordon is a software performance analyst for IBM, in Austin, Texas. He creates systems-level views of how software systems are put together and of how their components interact. These understandings make it possible for him to improve the software's performance.

Jesse joined IBM in 1990 after earning a B.A. in Mathematics from the University of Pennsylvania and a Ph.D. in Computer Science from the University of Michigan. Between undergraduate and graduate school, he worked for three years as a software systems analyst for BDM International in McLean, Virginia.

DON GRAY

Don Gray works with manufacturers integrating people, processes and projects. This work involves everything from the people involved to the sensors to the production/process data. Don's been working as an independent consultant since 1984. He likes solving problems and working with people. He's currently working on a better understanding of how people interact in solving complex technical problems. Having taught general computing (both software and hardware) and application-specific classes, Don has a unique perspective on life (who else would write an article entitled "How to Kill a Software Company"?)

BRIAN GULINO

Brian Gulino builds databases and database-backed Websites. He works closely with several companies in southern California that do hardware integration, hardware design, and Web-based instruction.

PETER HARRIS

Deadlines, software bugs.
All are vanquished with a smile.
Coder treads lightly.

JOSEPH HOWARD

I am 39, and am currently a consultant. I have programmed computers from the age of 12, on PCs, UNIX, and mainframes, and I've led a number of relatively successful large and small projects. I am married with two children. I spent six years in the U.S. Army as a programmer, a barracks sergeant, and a medic. I paint, fix my boat, read history, and play the recorder (a Blockflute). I have a Bachelor of Science in Computer Science from NY Regents, and I am currently working on a master's degree in Computer Science.

Readers may note I don't mind making exploratory statements in a forum to sound out ideas. It's just a forum, a sandbox, to test and brainstorm what might be alternative thoughts with other thinkers. If everyone agrees at the outset, there is nothing to learn.

I do feel that historically successful leaders studied previously successful leaders. Many successful leaders wrote well about leadership.

KEVIN HUIGENS

Kevin Huigens is a principal consultant for a software management consulting firm. A graduate of the December 1993 PSL workshop, Kevin has nineteen years of experience in all aspects of software management: coding, testing, requirements analysis, project management, and more.

STEVEN D. JACKSON

Steven D. Jackson is principal management engineer at S. D. Jackson & Associates, an international management consulting organization specializing in assisting firms to substantially increase profits through internally driven process improvements. Steve has considerable experience in implementing quality system processes and has worked for more than thirty years in all aspects of engineering and project management.

An international speaker and author, Steve has developed and delivered many training courses on quality and management subjects. As a Certified Quality Auditor and Certified Quality Manager, Steve has taught certification preparation classes for local sections of the American Society for Quality. He holds a Bachelor of Science in Engineering/Business Management and a master's in Computer Science from Nova University in Ft. Lauderdale, Florida.

Steve enjoys backpacking in the mountains and is a competition handgun shooter.

JAMES JARRETT

James Jarrett is a lead software designer at Rockwell Automation in Cleveland, Ohio. Specializing in interaction design, requirements engineering, and object-oriented development, he leads teams to deliver products that delight their users. Jim thrives on being a catalyst in his organization, helping it move toward best practices and high-performance teams. With varied interests, including sociology, science policy, and digital media, he brings a multidisciplinary perspective and a strong intuitive sense to his work and his world.

BOB KING

I work with people on project teams to build and document the shared understanding needed to get projects started on the path to success. Specifically, I work with project managers to write statements of work, with analysts to facilitate requirements gathering and analysis, and with senior technical people to design the solution. I have more than twenty-one years of experience: in the first sixteen, working myself up and out of American Express, and in the last five, as an independent consultant.

DAVE KLEIST

Dave Kleist, always interested in the next challenge, has held a variety of positions in the IT field during the last sixteen years, including project manager, account manager, instructor, and developer. He's even conned a few unsuspecting editors into publishing articles that he's written. Currently, Dave is the technical architect in the North American Best Practices Lab for Adaytum, Inc.

HENRY KNAPP

Holding a B.A. and an M.S. from UCSD (1969, 1971), Henry Knapp went into software engineering full-time in 1981, after using computers to run complex simulations for a number of years. He has since led the development of computer games, order entry and billing systems, process control systems, signal processing systems, and operating system software in the U.S., Switzerland, and Taiwan. He currently leads a group that develops storage management software for the Solaris operating system.

BRIAN KNOPP

Brian Knopp has worked in the software industry for the past twelve years. His initial work was in DOS, but since 1994, he has developed Windows applications using Visual Basic against the three major SQL platforms. Recently, he has begun developing Web applications using ASP. He lives in Dallas with his wife and son, where he hopes that the Stars can finish better than they started.

Fredric Laurentine **www.laurentine.com**

Fredric Laurentine works with organizations of all sizes leading groups of people through laughter and ideas to a creative, more human future.

Pat McGee

Pat McGee has programmed for all of his adult life, in many different languages (including English), and for many different processors, large and small (including homo sapiens). Pat has written programs to do scientific modeling, process improvement, fraud detection, computer graphics, business systems, and embedded control systems, and to break other programs. He has led teams and has been called the "best boss" and the "worst boss" ever, though not on the same day or by the same person, yet.

Nate McNamara **www.conquerrsi.com**

Nate McNamara held a variety of software engineering roles before he suffered a severe repetitive strain injury (RSI) that interrupted his career. Fortunately, Nate is one of a handful of RSI victims who have completely recovered, and he has successfully resumed all of his pursuits. In addition to performing object-oriented and Web software development and training in the San Francisco Bay area, Nate now presents seminars on curing RSI. For more information, visit the Website listed above.

George Olsen

George Olsen, principal of Interaction by Design, has done award-winning user-experience design, information architecture, and Web development for start-ups, Hollywood studios, such as Disney, and Fortune 500 companies, including Nestle and Transamerica. In 1998, he was runner-up for Builder.com's Web Innovator of the Year award for cofounding The Web Standards Project. He has taught, written and spoken at numerous conferences about user-experience design issues.

Mark Passolt

Mark Passolt manages the development of advanced scientific 3D visualization and collaboration software at Schlumberger. The design and visualization of large technical databases is the thread running through most of his work with software over the last twenty years. He has a master's degree in Mathematics from the University of Wisconsin, Madison. Outside of work, Mark enjoys woodworking and dabbles in metalworking and stained glass.

Sue Petersen www.networkboy.com/suep

Sue Petersen is an anthropologist by training, a programmer by avocation, and a manager by necessity. She and her husband have owned and operated a small plumbing repair shop since 1979. Sue started programming in 1985, when she bought her first PC for the business. Unable to find a simple database for the business, she created one herself.

She started writing professionally in 1995, when she sold her first article to *Windows Tech Journal.* She wrote a regular book review column for *Visual Developer Magazine* for many years, and currently freelances for other publications as well.

Sue's main professional interests are database design, and software engineering and management. She is currently programming in a Win32/Delphi environment.

Dwayne Phillips

Dwayne Phillips has been a systems and computer engineer with the U.S. government since 1980. He has written articles for magazines such as *The C/C++ Users Journal* and *The Cutter IT Journal,* and is author of *The Software Project Manager's Handbook.* A native of Sweetwater, Louisiana, he has a Ph.D. in Electrical Engineering from Louisiana State University. He resides in Reston, Virginia, with his wife, Karen, and three sons.

Brian Richter

Brian Richter has been a professional software developer on Long Island for nineteen years. He started out writing video games, branched out into character generators and teleprompters, and now writes software for radars and air traffic control systems. Outside of work, he is an accomplished composer, pianist, and musician who performs in and directs musical events and shows on Long Island.

SHARON MARSH ROBERTS

Sharon Marsh Roberts works primarily with large corporations on financial systems projects. She originally worked on managing financial analysis and reporting, but she discovered the challenge of designing and implementing systems.

Sharon is currently helping launch a multi-organizational, multidisciplinary team at Pfizer to comply with a new FDA Rule, Financial Disclosure by Investigators. She is focused on the business processes of capturing disclosures from investigators and communicating status to both investigators and drug teams.

Sharon is president of Roberts Financial Systems, Inc. Her firm specializes in systems in financial analysis, operations, and management information. She designed and managed the implementation of a managed healthcare system for one of the nation's largest insurers. Her role is usually designer or facilitator. A recent successful project was the on-time delivery of a human resources system that began late. Her current projects have been impact analyses of Y2K issues and of other problems in the pharmaceutical industry.

As former chairman of the Independent Computer Consultants Association, her goal is to improve project expertise. She seeks to creatively blend the resources of corporations and their contractual partners to meet business needs.

Sharon received an M.B.A. from New York University in 1982 and an Advanced Professional Certificate from the same institution in 1985. Her bachelor's degree, from Bucknell University, is in Education and German. She is a C.P.A. and a member of the AICPA and the NYSSCPA.

Roberts Financial Systems, Inc., in Linden, New Jersey, serves clients across the U.S. and can be reached at (908) 862-4726.

Brett Schuchert

Brett Schuchert's most recent work has dealt with software architecture and with forming the chaos at the beginning of a project. He is a teacher, mentor, and consultant.

On and off since 1985, Brett has taught courses on subjects ranging from computer literacy to the formal analysis and design of software systems. He has also served as architect, technical lead, and individual contributor on several projects in several domains.

Stuart Scott

Stuart Scott is a principal consultant with Cambridge Technology Partners, where he helps teams design and carry out business transformation programs. He is based in New York City.

Dave W. Smith

Dave W. Smith has been taking on ambitious, and sometimes desperate, projects in Silicon Valley start-ups for the past twenty years. In his spare time, Dave tries to catch up on his e-mail.

Steve Smith

Steve Smith works at the intersection of people, management, and systems, helping organizations to become more productive.

Although most of Steve's career has been technical—starting in 1975 as a systems programmer—over the years, his context has widened. Today, Steve tackles the most difficult problem businesses face—managing technical people so they achieve results rather than merely justify and deploy the latest technology.

Steve is a consultant, author, speaker, and expert facilitator and coach who honors and enhances the wisdom that lies dormant in groups. Steve works as a technical architect for EMC, a manufacturer of intelligent storage systems, software, and services.

DANIEL STARR

Daniel Starr still dresses in ways that put people into chaos (these days, he's often seen in kilts, as befits his Irish ancestry). After some twenty-six years in the corporate world, during which he evolved from software developer to software architect, system architect, system architecture process architect, and generalist-reviewer-opinion-generator, finally reaching the position of Consulting Member of Technical Staff at Bell Laboratories, he's moving into writing and independent consulting. In addition to his work in system architecture, process, reviews, and retrospectives, he's writing a vast, sprawling novel about time travel and hair spray.

WAYNE STRIDER

Cofounder and vice president of Strider & Cline, Inc., an IT management consulting firm based in Kansas City, Missouri, Wayne's IT career spans twenty-seven years. He conducts project reviews, project retrospectives, and organizational assessments for information technology organizations. Wayne and his partner, Eileen Strider, annually cohost their successful Leaders' Forum.

PETE TERMAAT

Pete is the founder and sole employee of the Minneapolis consulting firm Up to Code, Inc., where he hopes someday to win "Employee of the Month." He enjoys the quest for quality software, whether playing the role of developer, tester, manager, writer, trainer, or consultant. After more than fifteen years in the world of software, he still finds it all so exciting he sometimes forgets to eat lunch.

PHIL TRICE

Born on Davis Island in Tampa Bay, nurtured among the brackish lagoons, saw palmetto woods of Florida through mystical awakening in New York City and maturing in the Sonoran Desert of Arizona. Philip has been an originary explorer bridging ways of ancient and modern teachings, arts and engineering, mystical and physical, and natural and technological. From a varied life path—seeker, martial artist, designer, healer, systems architect, entrepreneur—from seeking access to the magic of life to a deep journey through his own shadow and light—Thunder Panther now explores shamanic ways of Lover, Warrior, and Magician, weaving the Métis ways of his path of heart among the forests and waters of Northern Idaho.

Thunder Panther has founded NW Originary Arts to assist businesses and individuals through projects, consulting, workshops, and intensives; to balance the aspects of story, substance, concept, passion, and value; and to bridge the artificial and natural realms, to co-venture with Earth and Spirit in artful business, coevolving natural law and value. He can be reached at ThunderPanther@nworiginaryarts.org.

Bill Trierweiler

Bill Trierweiler has spent the last thirty years looking for those moments that offer the possibilities for congruent leadership. It has taken him from the peace movement to tenant organizing to union building to community development to software development to systems change. He left Community Organizing and Family Issues (COFI) to found the Five Freedoms Center for Congruent Leadership. He can be reached at btree@interaccess.com

Marianne Tromp

Marianne has been involved in scientific software development since 1982. In 2001, Marianne started a Software Process Improvement Network (SPIN) in Madison, Wisconsin. Marianne especially enjoys providing software engineers with tools, guidelines, processes, and coaching, to free them to do the work they most enjoy doing.

Jerry Weinberg www.geraldmweinberg.com

Jerry Weinberg has worked on transforming software organizations for more than forty years. He is author, coauthor, or editor of scores of articles and books that cover all phases of software development. Innovative as a systems thinker, Jerry's classic works include *Are Your Lights On?*, *The Psychology of Computer Programming*, and *An Introduction to General Systems Thinking*. Jerry's books on phases of the software life cycle include *Exploring Requirements, Rethinking Systems Analysis and Design, The Handbook of Walkthroughs, Inspections, and Technical Reviews,* and *General Principles of Systems Design.* His books on leadership include *Amplifying Your Effectiveness, Becoming a Technical Leader, The Secrets of Consulting, More Secrets of Consulting,* and the *Quality Software Management* four-volume series.

To many, Jerry is as well-known for his workshops for software leaders as he is for his books. Workshops include Problem Solving Leadership (PSL), the Congruent Organizational Change-Shop, and Systems Effectiveness Management (SEM). He is also a cofounder of the AYE Conference.

KAY WISE **TheWiseChoice.com**

Kay A. Wise, president of TheWiseChoice.com, has more than thirty years of leadership in business and technology, including years as software engineer, database administrator, entrepreneur, project manager, and program director. Kay now works full-time as a consultant, speaker, writer, and teacher, emphasizing the politics and practical issues of launching and steering change projects in technology-intensive environments.

PREFACE

Since *Roundtable on Project Management,* the first book in the *Roundtable* series, came out, we have received very favorable feedback from readers. People have said they appreciate the dialogue format and being able to read what the experts are talking about on SHAPE, Jerry Weinberg's online discussion forum.

This new *Roundtable* book, *Roundtable on Technical Leadership,* samples a different set of discussion threads from SHAPE. Nearly forty software developers, managers, and consultants contribute their advice, lessons, and experiences—and some confessions—about the tricks they've used, the ways they learn from and teach each other, and the ways they can become better professionals by accepting themselves as people. Each of these topics is a component of technical leadership: our ability to extend our technical skills to the people skills we need for every technical endeavor.

Being a technical leader doesn't require you to have some fancy title or to be approved in that role by management. But it does require you to understand how your use of tools and techniques affects the program, the product, and the productivity of those who work with you or follow you in maintenance.

From the sheer volume of discussion that made its way into this *Roundtable*, it's easy to see that there is no lack of creativity in the world of programming. That creativity can contribute to your technical leadership, depending on how it's applied. Sometimes, though, we get too creative in the way we get our work done. Follow this book's lively discussion of "stupid" programmer tricks to see if you recognize one of your own so-called clever tricks. I did.

Many of the discussions on SHAPE have centered on the facts and fallacies of technical leadership, especially with regard to the way leaders deal with people. There's the technologist who can't relate to human beings, the guru who knows all, the expert who mentors and teaches others, and the expert who can't or won't share his knowledge. In this SHAPE dialogue, the contributors discuss each of these personalities, and others, uncovering the myths and truths about what it really means to be a leader.

Regardless of the topic, the honesty and the humor these leaders bring to the table allow you to get a rare glimpse into the real life and psyche of technical leaders, from many industries and many walks of life. If you are a technical leader, you'll probably recognize yourself in these threads, and if you don't think you're a leader, you just may decide you'd like to become one.

February 2002 M.A.B.
Bath, New York

Series Preface

Since 1996, Jerry Weinberg has hosted a subscription-only Internet forum named SHAPE, for Software as a Human Activity Practiced Effectively. This book is part of a series that extracts and organizes material from more than a million words of SHAPE contributions.

To me, SHAPE is the Algonquin Round Table of systems development. For a period of years, Dorothy Parker, Alexander Woollcott, Heywood Broun, and Robert Benchley gathered for long lunches at the "round table" in the Algonquin Hotel in New York City. They would gossip, trade quips, and chatter. They'd talk about their work, and their work was better for it. They pushed each other by being worthy colleagues and worthy competitors. During those long lunches, seeds were sown that became columns, essays, and plays.

I am regularly struck by the quality of insight and advice that shows up on the SHAPE forum. The high quality of the writing matches the high quality of the content. I've found less wisdom in week-long expert training or in months-long mentoring than in one morning when I log in to read SHAPE.

Its power, I think, comes from

- the breadth of the participants' backgrounds
- the participants' depth as individuals

- the grace of the interplay between the participants
- the interplay itself

We are not a group of Manhattan writers—though a few of us write from the Big Apple—and the common discipline is systems (Jerry says software), not literature. However, the conversation certainly is literate, challenging, and enlightening. On SHAPE, there are dozens of authors, consultants, managers, and workers from every IT specialty and every kind of organization, spread over five continents. This community isn't available in my city, my school, or my company, and never has been. Like the Algonquin Round Table, SHAPE is a high-quality community that pushes one to do better—it pushed me to find the Algonquin analogy itself. SHAPE is a very big roundtable.

We Shapers are familiar with the entire existing canon of systems development. (In fact, we wrote some of it.) We don't limit ourselves, however; the conversation includes psychology, anthropology, operations management, math of various flavors, physics, science fact and fiction, history, music, literature, and training—of people, dogs, and even horses. Even better, we use our own experiences. Hanging about on SHAPE are a couple thousand years of system-building experience. This richness leads to tremendous "signal to noise"—part of Jerry's description of SHAPE. Whatever I read on SHAPE is relevant, informed, and always worth my time.

Building systems is, I think, one of the hardest, most human activities. Why spend hours discussing hard problems on the SHAPE forum, with people who can't advance your career—and who don't even pay you? For me, the joy of the association and of what I learn is reason enough. I believe the Algonquin Round Table made those writers' work better. To do my work, I need all the help I can get.

SHAPE supports my urge to get better at this thing I do—yet I think it's bigger than that. Systems come from individual experts inventing and creating in concert, rather like SHAPE itself. As the useful objects in our world are less made of "stuff" and more made of "thought," more activities become like building systems—people creating by thinking together, versus *making* together. (That's just my opinion. Some folks on SHAPE will disagree, but that's okay. We'll talk about it.)

The Internet enables communities that are independent of space and time. The Internet lowers the cost and expands the reach of each community's vanity press. Some social critics argue that "Net addiction" attracts people who lack social skills and have nothing to say. I wouldn't know about that. I've become addicted to a community of people with more insight and grace than I have found by any other means. The wired world allows a small minority to reach critical mass by having access to more people, across broader time. I've found a community of sincere intention (a phrase I learned from SHAPE) that is also a living example of what it takes to build good systems. It's the people thing, not the Net thing, that matters to me.

I wanted to extend this community even further, so I asked about it on SHAPE:

How do we share this with the rest of the world?

Jerry replied: "I often think about that question. After all, we Shapers are trying to change the world."

What we've done—Marie Benesh and Jerry and I—is take part of two years' worth of the discussions and *shaped* the threads into a series of books. The shaping process was mainly a matter of organizing what people posted on the forum. It really couldn't be any other way. After all, how could a few of us duplicate or even represent two millennia of refined experience? We didn't even try.

March 2001
Seattle

J.B.

ROUNDTABLE ON TECHNICAL LEADERSHIP

A SHAPE Forum Dialogue

INTRODUCTION

The two most common elements in the universe are hydrogen and stupidity.

The Threads

JERRY WEINBERG

At one point, SHAPE had a thread about responsibility for Y2K problems. I don't think we settled the question, but the whole Y2K issue raised another issue in my mind: This whole mess stemmed from the idea of "saving two bytes, or two digits." Back in 1956, when I started as a programmer, saving two digits was a rather clever trick. In some cases, we even used a single digit for the year, which, when your machine has a total data storage of about 100 digits, is truly clever.

But, when your machine has 100 million digits of data storage, truncated dates become a rather stupid programmer trick. And, over the years, it's not the only trick that has become (or always was) stupid. Here's another one: dynamically modifying a subroutine (or object, or data item) to improve its behavior, then modifying it back when my program is finished using it. This works if nobody else uses the subroutine in the meantime and if the memory layout hasn't been changed, so everything remains in the same, absolute locations. If these conditions don't hold (and they often don't), the result of this trick is an unmitigated disaster.

With these tricks in mind, I started a thread called Stupid Programmer Tricks, with the following questions:

1. What's your favorite stupid programmer trick?
2. Why is it stupid?
3. What can be done to prevent it?

Of course, as soon as I posed these questions, my cyberspace conscience, Sue Petersen, had to respond.

Sue Petersen
I like the thread, but I must say the title grates on me. It must be a little too close to home.

Jerry Weinberg
Should I call it "Brilliant Programmer Tactics"? A lot of these tricks are thought to be brilliant—by their perpetrators. Anyway, I'll extend this thread to include truly clever programmer tricks.

So, here are some new questions for this thread:

1. What's your favorite clever programmer trick?
2. Why is it clever?
3. What can be done to encourage it?
4. What must be done to keep it from turning into a stupid programmer trick?

The totality of these tricks will be something of a primer for the would-be technical leader who leads primarily through action. As the child's verse goes,

You're making a Gospel,
A chapter a day,
By things that you do,
And things that you say.

The replies to these questions supplied a full five chapters of technical leader Gospel in this book, with a lot left over for other books.

Yet, after composing those five chapters, I realized that I didn't want to leave the impression that technical leadership was simply a matter of doing clever things and avoiding stupid things.

What else was there? Well, on a second thread, a number of Shapers had a great deal to say about the behavior of experts and gurus—especially about their teaching methods—and that discussion contributed three more chapters. But this Gospel, too, would have been misleading without some lessons from another thread, on an expert's courage to act on expert knowledge or self-knowledge.

Taken all together, these three threads give dozens of examples of real technical leadership. I consider them an ideal supplement to my earlier book *Becoming a Technical Leader.*[1]

[1] Gerald M. Weinberg, *Becoming a Technical Leader: An Organic Problem-Solving Approach* (New York: Dorset House Publishing, 1986).

1

Tricks That Ignore Those Who Come After

The Thread

Here again are our questions:

1. *What's your favorite clever programmer trick?*
2. *Why is it clever?*
3. *What can be done to encourage it?*
4. *What must be done to keep it from turning into a stupid programmer trick?*

—Jerry Weinberg

Hard-Coding Information That Will Change in the Future

SUE PETERSEN

My favorite stupid programmer trick is hard-coding information that will change in the future. It must be my favorite, I get bit so often.

I don't know if it's stupid to hard-code a value when I'm first sketching out an idea. If I take time to "do it right" before my ideas have settled, I'll get sidetracked with issues that aren't directly relevant to the problem at hand. But it's definitely stupid if I forget, or don't bother, to go back and "do it right" after the design has stabilized.

I don't know how to prevent myself from doing this. Making sure I remind myself that it's important, making notes (sometimes embedding "hack alert" comments in the code). Peer reviews, of course, would help, if I had somebody nearby who wanted to trade reviews.

JERRY WEINBERG

Some compilers can be set to disallow constants of any kind. I don't know if any that you use can be set that way.

SUE PETERSEN

Nope. Actually, constants aren't that big a problem in my environment; the *real* trouble is when I start embedding special cases in the code. For instance, we're a very small company. The president gets paid on a salary basis, and everyone else is paid commission. So, I slipped a special case into the payroll routine to keep it from cluttering up that particular screen with the hours the president billed. But then we hired an apprentice who's paid for hours worked, regardless of hours billed—so *his* hours shouldn't be on that screen either, since they're calculated on a separate time sheet.

JERRY WEINBERG
But you'd need some sort of constant to identify which person is the president. The right compiler could flag that and give you your hack alert automatically.

SUE PETERSEN
The next time I do a rewrite, I'll fold that logic into an INI file or something else that lets me maintain it in data instead of code. It's not terribly hard to do, because my code *is* modular. But if I'd done it right the first time, I wouldn't have to worry about it now.

Except, when I wrote that code the first time, I had no idea we'd end up with a system in which people are paid differently, depending on their status. How much time should I waste trying to think of remote possibilities? When is a "stupid trick" really worth the time you save? And how on earth do you tell the difference? These are difficult questions.

Failing to Clean Up Temporary Code

JERRY WEINBERG
Sue mentioned a second stupid trick: not taking the time to clean up various scaffolding, or temporary, junk in your code.

Years ago, our studies of error-prone code modules revealed one almost certain predictor of code that was costly to use and maintain. That predictor was the occurrence of the string TEMP somewhere in the finished code.

We surmised that TEMP indicated a programmer in too much of a hurry to do the right thing and go back and clean up the code, or even in too much of a hurry to think it through in the first place. We calculated that the average TEMP in this particular operating system cost the company about $85,000 in its lifetime—that is, the amount of maintenance work in these error-prone modules divided by the number of TEMP strings. What it cost the users is anybody's guess.

Making Comments Impossible to Ignore

Joseph Howard

One of my favorite stupid tricks is the use of magic words as tags for the preprocessing in compilers. This trick is particularly common in C++.

I'd define a magic word as a special tag word that is used to indicate code that should only be changed by the preprocessor. Many of these magic words look like user-modifiable code macros or comments, but are really language constructs outside the language. Some tags are unmodifiable and undocumented macros; some are documented macros; and some are marker comments in the same language implementation.

A tag cannot be moved or changed safely without using the wizard that embedded the tag. Try finding and fixing a changed tag that is implemented as a comment (the compiler won't tell what is wrong). When your comment matches a comment tag, a warning doesn't necessarily appear. For example,

> Is /*AAddButton*/ a comment or a magic tag?
> How about //AFXBUTTON or //} } AFX_DATA_INIT?

Microsoft, among others, uses these magic words for its C++ class wizard. Microsoft generally warns the user not to modify the code with comments, but some things (like adding an option to a menu bar) will require changing this tagged code.

There was really no need to invent magic words in C++. With a class wizard that is a little smarter about its API and classes, the compiler can change the behavior of the code that the tag stands for, without needing tags.

These tags are the usually poorly documented part of the API that makes learning a new language a much harder job.

Out in bookstores, for those who like this topic, is *The Unix Hater's Handbook.* A very fine whine.

JERRY WEINBERG
Perhaps we could generalize the stupidity of this trick. *Any* action that makes comments something that you cannot safely ignore, if you wish, is stupid. It means that your comments are not comments.

Overloading the Value of an Identifier

JIM BATTERSON
And for a stupid analyst trick, I offer the following example:

We were designing a system that assigned customer numbers and produced various reports. Sometimes the users wanted the reports sorted by customer number, but other times it was better for them to sort the reports by customer name. Certain reports were to be produced twice, one sorted by number and one sorted by name.

So, we hit upon the brilliant idea of assigning customer numbers based on name so that a single report would be sorted both alphabetically and numerically. Initially, we just sorted the whole list by name and assigned numbers in order, leaving appropriate gaps for future additions. When we needed to enter a new customer, we could do a binary search, find just the right slot, and assign a new customer number that would preserve the order.

What went wrong? Did I mention that these were commercial customers? That the record sequence would change when companies changed their names or were bought out by other customers? Or that Wal-Mart alone had roughly a thousand customer numbers, one for every location, and the gaps we left were nowhere near big enough?

So, when a company changed its name, we would create a stub record with the old customer name and number, pointing to the new record with the new name and the newly assigned number.

Jerry Weinberg
Ah, the fatal first glass of beer!

Jim Batterson
This was all done programmatically and was nearly transparent to the users. Over time, we created "chains" for a customer, pointing from an original number to a second, which pointed to a third, and so on.

The programming required to support this scheme infused every program with an additional level of complexity. Simple changes became complex, simple reports took longer to create. Under certain circumstances, it was possible to create networks of customer numbers. When two customers merged into one or when one split into two, we would have to choose one. We have had programming errors that created loops from chains, so that record A pointed to record B which pointed to C which pointed back to A. This system still exists, and I thank God I am no longer working on it.

This trick is stupid because we were overloading the value of customer number with way too much meaning. An identifier, such as a customer number, should be used simply as an identifier.

A reasonable solution is to provide one database index by customer number and another one by name, and to allow your users to browse online by whichever key they want. And never assign too much meaning to a field. Live and learn.

Overloading the Mind of the Writer or the Reader

James Bullock
There's a more general principle at work here. A notation convention has to have enough categories for the kinds of things in the system. The stupid programmer trick is to get limited by syntax. Don't overload something with multiple meanings or

multiple ways of behaving. Instead, invent something that looks different.

Jerry Weinberg
I'll buy that. What you overload is the mind of anyone trying to understand the code, including the person who wrote it originally.

Creating Cryptic or Cute Variable Names

Dave Kleist
My favorite stupid programmer trick: when people use short, cryptic, or cute variable names, as if they're completing a homework assignment instead of a professional task.

Jerry Weinberg
Yes, yet another way of overloading the human mind.

This one is great when the program grows and programmers start reusing the same names for different reasons. I once debugged (partially—the whole job was impossible) a program that used PAT three times: once when the programmer was using women's names, once when he was using three-letter acronyms from the application itself, and once when he was using football terms.

Using One Argument to Change the Meaning of Another

Peter Harris
I once worked with a man who would use a negative number in one argument to change the semantic meaning of another argument. He did this "to save stack space." As you might expect, the resultant code was impenetrable, especially by the third layer of subroutines down (each of which performed this little optimization). Happy birthday!

Jerry Weinberg
What a lovely birthday present, Peter. It fills me with delight that I don't have to decipher this kind of code anymore, at my age. At least he used subroutines, so he wasn't writing those

incomprehensible, unmaintainable, long code segments. He was writing incomprehensible, unmaintainable, short code segments. Quite a triumph!

Naming with Too Much (or Too Little) English

Jerry Weinberg

Choosing names is a psychological problem, and there's much literature to bear on the choosing of names. For one thing, people don't read really long words—they just pick up the first one or two letters, the length, and perhaps the ending letter. We did experiments with those long COBOL names required by certain standards and found that people made *beaucoup* mistakes by failing to discriminate among, say,

```
ABC_PAYROLL_PERSONAL_DEDUCTIONS_00001
ABC_PAYROLL_PERSONAL_DEDUCTIONS_40001
ABC_PAYROLL_SEASONAL_DEDUCTIONS_00001
```

In other words, length (both too much and too little of it) hurts when precision is required. I'm not sure that English is a good model of the kind of precise language we need in computer programming. "Looks like English" is the source of many, many stupid programmer tricks (when it doesn't quite *act* like English, or when English isn't very clear on what it means).

James Bullock

As for symbol length, English isn't great. And I'll admit to being a happy user of APL, Lisp, and Forth, which all look and act pretty different from English. I'll also admit that I do most of my thinking about a program in terms of communicating sequential processes, functional expressions, data flows, or relations.

But, if we're stuck with something we have to read top-down, left-to-right, with "execution steps" and such, I'd rather see syntax that's something like this:

```
Case (Coil_Output_Temperature <
    Efficiency_Limit(External_Ambient, Coil_Input_Temperature))

Compressor_Output_Target :=
    Control_Loop(SetPoint_Temperature,
    Indoor_Ambient_Temperature)

Else (Coil_Output_Temperature <
    Superheat_Limit(External_Ambient))

Compressor_Output_Target :=
    Efficiency_Model_Limit(Control_Loop
    (Setpoint_Temperature Indoor_Ambient_Temperature)

Else
    Compressor_Output_Target:=
    Superheat_Exception_Output

EndCase
```

I'd prefer that to something like this:

Case (t3 > f21(t5, t7) . . . and so on.

JERRY WEINBERG
Actually, I find the first case rather difficult to follow. I think there's something in between those two that's more reasonable than either—for example, abbreviations that would be meaningful to any engineer in the appropriate field. The stupid trick is going to either extreme.

Casting Types: Smart or Stupid?

JAMES BULLOCK
Casual type casting is a phenomenally stupid trick that has been canonized into law. To avoid this trick, you should either

- have types that are distinct, and never the twain shall meet
- work out a generic "wrapper" that hides the gymnastics
- work out a data structure that does what you really want, and use it

So, in terms of stupid tricks (sorry, this is flame-bait here), Hungarian notation is right up there, for me at least. I don't want to have the type dragging around in the symbol name. Type conversion needs to be explicit, hard, and hidden. The only reason to drag the type around is to make sure that two things have conformable types when they should. But don't you know that? Shouldn't you know? Shouldn't the compiler/linker/environment help you out with this? (Not if it's C with errors suppressed, it won't.)

Building Monolithic Code

Dwayne Phillips
One trick I've suffered through is putting all the code in one subroutine or in the main program. People concentrating on (notice I didn't say "obsessed with") performance do this because subroutine calls slow down execution. Sometimes execution speed is the highest priority, but I have never seen it as that important.

Jerry Weinberg
Yes, this is another overloading trick, and part of a large collection of stupid programmer tricks that come under the heading of "optimization." Of course, if you analyze the dynamics of large, unmodifiable hunks of code over their lifetime, you find that the end result is almost always poorer performance.

Dave Kleist
At my current client site, the quotable line is "That's awfully complicated, can't you put that into one program?" (Real quote, and no, I didn't put it all into one program). I've seen them do it because it's too hard to break apart once they build

up a head of steam. They don't do any up-front design, so the monster builds until it's too late. It becomes a snarled mess, like a Kevlar version of the Gordian knot.

Jerry Weinberg
Well, Alexander knew how to solve this one. Perhaps that's why he was called "The Great."

Dwayne Phillips
What's the problem with one great big routine? Nothing, as long as it works. If, however, there is something wrong (and it seems that clever programmers cannot imagine having something wrong with one of their programs), it is incredibly hard to find and fix.

Dave Kleist
Steve McConnell says, "If you don't know why it works, it probably doesn't. You just don't know it yet."

I've never seen a huge module that ever really worked right: The clever programmers just fix the faults that cause big failures. They can't ever prove it really works, because the number of execution paths is too large to imagine, much less verify.

Jerry Weinberg
The most ambiguous noun/pronoun in English is "it." One of the most ambiguous verbs is "work." Put them together, and what do you get? "It works." This might be okay if we knew what "it" was and what it meant to "work," but those who say this never know either.

Dwayne Phillips
Prevention is simple yet impossible: coding standards that disallow long routines and encourage peer reviews. The trouble is getting people to allow such activities.

Dave Kleist
I think it's more fundamental than that. It's getting people to know why they don't want to do things in the first place. Sadly, most still don't know why.

Dwayne Phillips
Some people will not tolerate anyone looking at their work. We must kindly tell them that such intolerance is not permitted at work.

Jerry Weinberg
Or, at least, cannot be permitted in certain lines of work. If they want to have their own private code, then perhaps they can find employment at an organization that doesn't care about fraud or failure. I'm sure there are some such organizations like that somewhere, though I can't think of any at the moment.

Disregarding the Difficulty of Maintenance

Brian Knopp
James Bullock offered some flame-bait on type casting, so get out your asbestos underwear! There's one other good reason to "drag the type around," and it is this: to simplify the job of the poor schmuck who has to come after you and maintain your code. If self-interest will help, consider that *you* are often the aforementioned "poor schmuck." Or, at least, I have been that schmuck on more occasions than I care to remember.

James Bullock
What are the chances of getting "Poor Schmuck Support" past a product review? You can imagine the discussion: "Who are the customers for this new feature?" "Oh, they're the poor schmucks who actually use the thing." Doesn't sound good.

Jerry Weinberg
Yes, but the companies who have this kind of PSS aren't likely to have an effective product review process anyway.

James Bullock
An old mantra of mine, from an organization that was changing the way it built systems (as they realized that they were building systems), goes like this: "We need to make it easy for people to do the stuff we want and hard for them to do the stuff we don't want. That way, everything will get better."

Fortunately, this organization needed to get stuff done, so we were able to tweak the environment any way that helped.

Unfortunately, I learned later in life that actually making things better isn't always the goal. Some folks complain, because they think that is their job. If what they're complaining about actually improves, they've got to think up something else, and that's work. Some folks believe that if we make programmers' jobs (and those held by line workers, sales folks, call center folks, and so on) "easier," the programmers (and others) won't be "earning their money." There is some perverse attraction to the ability to make people miserable.

So, I would suggest a meta-level stupid programmer trick: staying in a nonsensical organization. One without an interest in PSS. One that makes everything difficult.

The Poor Schmuck Prayer might be in order:

Lord, grant me the tools to keep me out of stupid trouble,
the genius to do the hard stuff,
and the perspective to know which is which.

Lessons

Jerry Weinberg

All of the tricks in this chapter are kinds of false economies: The original developer does things that seem easy but actually create more work. This may seem wise in the rush to meet a development schedule, but it creates costs that continue throughout the life of the software. After all, a program is generally read many, many times more often than it's written.

1. When you take a shortcut, embed an indicator—a hack alert—to find it later.
2. Take the time to clean up all the hack alerts. You're not really done until they're gone.
3. Don't overload a single symbol, syntax, or notation with multiple meanings or behaviors—invent something that looks and feels different.
4. People need to know *why* they don't want to do things in the first place. Sadly, most still don't know why.
5. Include "Poor Schmuck Support" in the program, and in the environment. The poor schmuck may be you.
6. Use all the diagnostics and alerts in the development environment—they are there for a reason.
7. Make it easy for people to do the stuff we want them to do, and hard for them to do the other stuff. That way, we'll get more of the good stuff.

2

Tricks That Destroy Portability

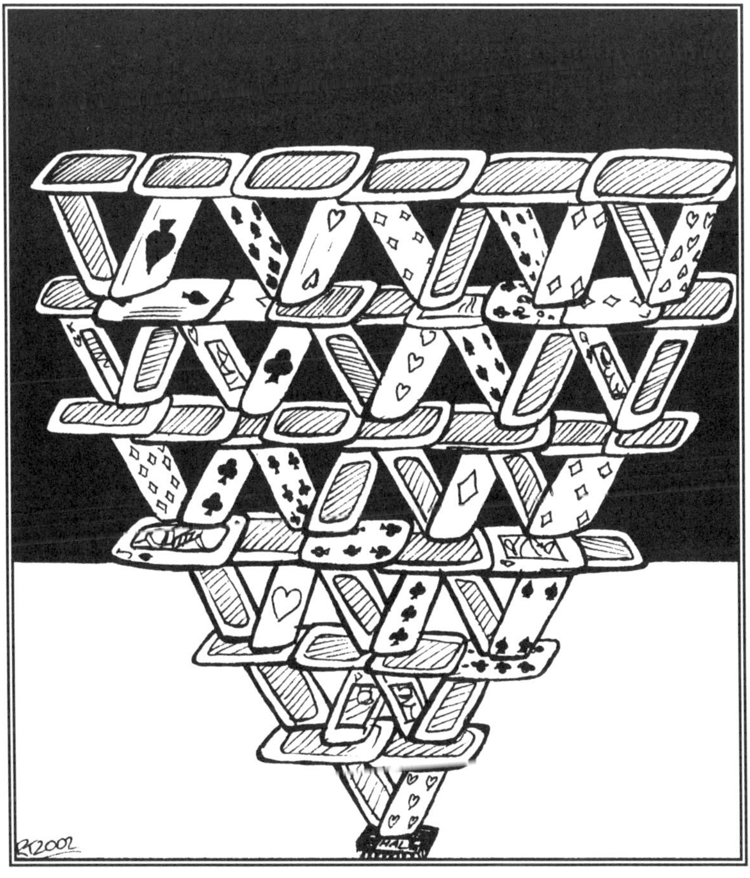

The Thread

Here, we continue our discussion of stupid tricks and how to prevent them, especially those that are most tempting when writing code.

—Jerry Weinberg

Embedding Machine Dependencies in What Looks Like Portable Code

DANIEL STARR

My all-time favorite stupid trick was something I ran into in some C code I inherited from a certain world-famous software expert who shall remain nameless.

This guy had written a small system to control a PBX. Buried within it was a little task-dispatching routine that wrote into an automatic array with a negative subscript (that is, a [-4]), and then returned. What he was actually doing was overwriting the return address on the stack, so that when he hit the return instruction, control would transfer to his routine.

It seems the reason for this trick was to avoid dropping into assembly language to manipulate the program counter directly. Clever, eh?

In the more general sense, this trick is called "embedding machine dependencies in what looks like portable code." Remember that the whole selling point of C, back in those days, was its machine independence. But this trick will only work on a computer that has a particular stack arrangement, and then only if the compiler has a particular method for defining automatic arrays within a stack frame. As you might guess, I found this trick while trying to port the code to a different computer, one that had a somewhat different stack arrangement.

Jerry Weinberg
Even worse is when the system *sometimes* uses the same stack arrangement.

Daniel Starr
What can be done to prevent it? In this case, given the stature of the person who committed this trick, and his association with the idea of portability in software, I think public humiliation would have been enough (not that this was likely to happen in our company—being a newbie, I just gritted my teeth and kept quiet about the whole business).

In the larger sense, I think we need to keep in mind the purpose of our clever programming concepts like portability. The purpose of a portable language is to allow people to move code easily from one machine to another.

Jerry Weinberg
Well, *more* easily, anyway.

Daniel Starr
There are times when you have to accept machine dependencies, and on those occasions, you should recognize that the best way to support easy porting is to follow these steps: Put a big red flag in front of the machine-dependent stuff, explain clearly what it does, and make it clear that when the code is ported, this part should be rewritten from the specification.

Depending on the Permanence of Message Texts

Daniel Starr
Dave Kleist mentioned "cute variable names." I just gotta relate the story of a really cute name I saw in a program, especially since it related to me. Way back when, I led a group that made an operating system for a real-time control system. For a bit of levity, I started putting humorous (at least to me) start-up messages in each new lab release. One of these messages offended an application developer, who promptly devoted his life to expunging that message from the OS. He wrote a rou-

tine that searched all of the memory for the offending phrase, and buried in that routine was this label:

DEATHSTARR

I laughed myself silly when I found it in his code—which we were inspecting in the lab because he had made the stupid programmer mistake (not a stupid programmer trick) of not considering how his loop would terminate if it never found what it was looking for. His search routine had coincided with my next release, which had a different message.

JERRY WEINBERG
So, once again, portability was destroyed by assuming that the details of one version would remain the same in later versions—in this case, the message text. Both this and the previous trick are stupid because they link things that are only accidentally linked—there is no reason in the application or the design for these connections, so they are unlikely to be preserved across implementations or versions, nor are they likely to be noticed before they cause trouble.

Inventing Your Own Programming Language

DANIEL STARR
This guy was fired, but not for "DEATHSTARR." While finding his mistake, we also happened upon another great stupid programmer trick—the guy had dedicated the last several months to building his own private programming language, using the macro facility! Even if his code had worked (which it didn't), the stuff would have been completely unmaintainable, since nobody else would have understood his language.

I still shudder when I read the things by Kernighan and Ritchie that tout the C compiler's macro facility (saying, essentially, "Hey, you can make your C code look like FORTRAN with just a few hundred `#define` macros!"). I never understood why they thought this was a good idea.

Jerry Weinberg

Inventing your own language may be the stupidest programmer trick of all. It falls in a class of tricks that say, in effect, "The present environment is not good enough, so I will invent a modification that will ensure that we'll never be able to move this code to another environment without the maximum amount of trouble."

Depending on Internal Compiler Details

Jim Batterson

There's an old COBOL trick of clearing a table using "propagation."

First, you define a table like this:

```
01 CLEAR-TABLE.
02 FILLER PIC S9(7) COMP-3 VALUE ZEROS.
02 TABLE.
03 TABLE-ENTRY PIC S9(7) COMP-3 OCCURS 1000.
```

Then you can clear all occurrences of TABLE-ENTRY by coding this:

```
MOVE CLEAR-TABLE TO TABLE.
```

This works because the move statement moves one byte at a time from left to right and overlays itself as it goes.

When I first saw this trick, I thought it was the niftiest thing I had ever seen. I used it a lot and passed it on to my friends. The alternative required a paragraph with a MOVE ZERO to an entry, which was performed by varying an index.

It has been many years since I coded in COBOL, but my recollection is that this technique did not work with subsequent compiler releases that used the move-long assembler instruction for tables above a certain size (512 bytes?). In any case, it was a bad technique because it depended on an understanding of the internal implementation methods of the compiler, which were subject to change. It was also obscure, and many programmers did not understand what it was doing.

A subsequent version of COBOL featured an INITIALIZE verb that made the technique obsolete. As a more general rule, one should not take advantage of internal implementation methods of the compiler.

Jerry Weinberg

Once again, we resort to this type of trick because we find the particular system unsatisfactory—but in the end, these tricks tie us to the same system because they don't port well.

Sue Petersen

You're talking about compilers here, but I think the principle applies in life as well. We make adjustments to live in an uncomfortable situation, and those adjustments make it less likely that we'll be able to create and/or function in a healthy environment.

Jerry Weinberg

James Bullock's meta-level stupid programmer trick—"staying in a nonsensical organization"—is one special case of Sue's more general stupid human trick. Once again, it's the story of Levine the Genius Tailor: Seeing a man trying to adjust his posture to a terribly tailored suit, a stranger says, "Levine must be a genius to fit a cripple like you."[1] If the suit doesn't fit, don't wear it.

Using Half-Significant Things That Could Become Significant

Daniel Starr

Here's another stupid programming trick (should I start worrying about the fact that I can come up with so many of these, so quickly?):

The compiler my team was using accepted identifier names with an arbitrary number of characters, but only viewed the

[1] Gerald M. Weinberg, *The Secrets of Consulting* (New York: Dorset House Publishing, 1985), pp. 42–43.

first six as significant, ignoring the rest. So, in the interest of making our code more readable, we started using long, meaningful identifiers rather than cryptic six-character ones.

There are at least two reasons why this trick is stupid. The obvious one is that two people could define identifiers that are the same in their first six characters and different beyond that point. As far as the compiler is concerned, these two programmers are talking about the same thing, so the values of the variables change mysteriously once the program is running. This turns out to be a minor problem, because

1. Modularity and scope tend to reduce the number of people whose identifiers are seen at one time (pretty much reducing this problem to only global variables).

Jerry Weinberg
But notice how one stupid trick can interact nonlinearly with another (in this case, with monolithic programs).

Daniel Starr

2. You tend to catch this kind of trick in early development and integration, before customers get the product.

The second reason is more subtle. After several years of developing, maintaining, and modifying this code, we moved to a new compiler that viewed the first *eight* characters of an identifier name as significant. We got hundreds of compilation and linking errors, where it turns out that the identifiers `stupid1` and `stupidl` (digit versus letter in the seventh character position) are now perceived as distinct.

What do we do with this? Do we assume that `stupid1` and `stupidl` are the same thing, and the mismatch is just a typo that we can fix automatically? Or are we in fact uncovering a lurking error, that `stupid1` and `stupidl` were *supposed* to be distinct, accidentally became the same, and we just so far haven't encountered the specific set of input conditions that makes this error blow things up?

JERRY WEINBERG
This is part of a large class of tricks that are short-sighted and fail to acknowledge that seemingly immutable things change. Older programmers tend not to make this kind of mistake because of the following two facts:

1. They've seen immutable things change before and have been caught.
2. They learned. If they didn't learn, they're no longer around. They're not immutable either.

DANIEL STARR
How did we prevent this trick? For once, it's something simple, and it ties in with the earlier remarks about preprocessors and comments: The language and its tools must clearly mark the boundary between what is processed and what is ignored. In other words, if the compiler sees six significant characters, then it should view a seventh character as an error condition. Stuff that is not intended to be read by the compiler should be stuck within comment markers, period. Stuff that is in the machine-readable part of the program should be read by the machine. No gray areas allowed!

JERRY WEINBERG
And the source listing should make the difference abundantly clear, which prevents other problems, such as unclosed comments that capture what you thought was executable code.

DANIEL STARR
One of the interesting things about the C language spec is that it doesn't say how many characters an identifier should have; that's an implementation detail. Seems to me that this is a strange omission for a portable language. The situation I described above (which happened on a big project) is not as bad as the reverse—when the new compiler recognizes *fewer* significant characters. If you're lucky, you get "variable redeclared" messages all over the place; if not, well, good luck making that stuff run.

Arbitrarily Limiting a Tool's Capacity

JAMES BULLOCK
I'm not so convinced that using long identifiers is the stupid trick. I think maybe limiting the size of a significant identifier is the stupid trick. What does this actually save? Compile time? Compile memory? What's the trade-off?

DANIEL STARR
Beats me. The point I was making is that the number of characters allowed in the source code and the number recognized by the compiler were different, which created all sorts of problems when identifiers were only unique in the characters ignored by the compiler. I personally prefer long, meaningful identifiers. But in any case, I think the number recognized and the number allowed should be the same.

JERRY WEINBERG
Making the used size and the seen size different was the stupid trick. But arbitrarily limiting the size of identifiers is a stupid trick on the part of the compiler and/or language designer.

These tricks let the machine architecture peek through a system that's supposedly hardware independent.

Optimizing for Something You've Got Lots Of

JAMES BULLOCK
True story: During cross-assembly, we got a new version of the assembler (which was written in FORTRAN itself, but that is another issue), and someone asked, "How big should we make the symbols?"

I immediately asked how big they could get. The answer was 255. "How about 255?" I suggested.

"You'll never see that many characters in a name."

"Okay, why not eighty—the width of a screen?"

"It will take up too much memory!"

"Well, how much is too much, and why?"

We eventually compromised on 32 (powers of 2 were attractive for some reason I never did understand), and I didn't have to worry about variables silently overloading each other. We could use big names and make the code look like English.

There are times when it's necessary to optimize for compile time, or some such. But not most of the time. This distinction relates to a stupid trick in general: optimizing for something we've got lots of. As we've said before, since we read code more than we write it, over the life of the system, maybe we should optimize for reading, not for writing.

Jerry Weinberg

Optimizing often depends on details that are unique to the hardware and the compiler. To that extent, it's also another portability trap. What's optimized for one environment is often pessimized for another.

Ignoring Compiler Warnings

Daniel Starr

Jerry wrote, *"And the source listing should make the difference abundantly clear, which prevents other problems, such as unclosed comments that capture what you thought was executable code."*

I had the privilege of working with such a compiler a long, long time ago, and I remember a number of occasions when the following message really saved my butt:

```
COMMENT CONTAINS /* — STATEMENTS MAY BE LOST
```

Of course, I can count the number of compilers that did this on the fingers of one finger.

Jerry Weinberg

I beg to differ: The *message* didn't save your butt; *paying attention to the message* saved it. One of the stupidest programmer tricks is to ignore compiler (or execution) warnings, under the model that "they're only warnings."

James Bullock

There's a stupid trick: suppressing error messages, from any tool—compiler, linker, loader, run-time environment handler, OS, DBMS Server, Object Broker, and so on. You can ignore any error message you get, but it's hard to react to the ones you never see.

The argument I usually get about suppressing error messages goes like this: "But I'm doing this big, mysterious thing that the compiler really doesn't understand." I haven't found one yet where there isn't a construct that does the job at least as well, and doesn't generate errors or warnings. Usually, the error-message-free way to do it has some uncommon syntax. So, the real problem is that the programmer wanted to do something odd, *without making it look different.* But it *is* different so it *ought to* look different.

Jerry Weinberg
There's that principle again.

Lacking—or Ignoring—Information from the Compiler

Jerry Weinberg
Back to type casting. Years ago, we experimented with using Chinese characters as data names, because they could easily carry more information—but the technology of that time didn't really support it. I still think Chinese is better than Hungarian, for this purpose. Again, a problem with Hungarian and such notations is that what you see is not necessarily bound by the compiler, so it's not a reliable indicator of type. The programmer has to be disciplined and consistent (not a bad idea, but hard to practice perfectly).

Brian Knopp
"The programmer has to be disciplined and consistent." A true statement, Jerry, irrespective of the compiler technology.

Jerry Weinberg
A way to reconcile this difference and put less strain on the programmer's memory would be to use a good compiler that tacks the type onto the identifiers in the source listing when there is a conversion, as in the following (in no particular language):

```
x{integer} := y{float} + z{fixed decimal}
```

This would make conversions explicit and would give the maintainer the information needed. At the same time, it wouldn't clutter the listing with information that isn't needed when there are no conversions taking place. I don't know of any compilers that do this, though many of them give warnings if a conversion is forced—and many programmers ignore those warnings.

Brian Knopp
I like the idea of tacking the type onto the identifiers in the source, although giving a compiler the sophistication required to identify when conversions are taking place and when they're not could prove challenging. I'd probably want the type information shown all the time. Of course, that could be put under programmer control with an environment switch.

Jerry Weinberg
I think the compiler should know this already, as it's going to supply the code to do the conversions.

Brian Knopp
I don't know of any compilers that tack the type onto the identifiers, although I'm hopeful that this will appeal to any vendors lurking in the SHAPE forum. As we mentioned earlier, ignoring compiler warnings certainly qualifies as a stupid programmer's trick of the first water.

Jerry Weinberg
We'll add your vote to that trick. It's very, very common, especially when the compiler gives several levels of error message. The lower levels don't sound so bad, compared with the higher, so the programmers ignore them. "Did you get a clean compile?" "Yeah, just a couple of warning messages. No *fatal* errors."

Depending on the Compiler to Be Consistent Across Environments

JOSEPH HOWARD
I like the idea of compiler-denoted typing, but having long declarations in-line makes the code harder to read, especially for complex data types. (Microsoft and other compilers allow the developer to see the reference and declaration, which is better.)

I never trust the compiler for these compiler-decided conversions. Some compilers do convert for you. All type conversions should be coded explicitly as a good practice. If I were to code it that way, I would make the fact of the conversion obvious to the developer following me. The compiler should disallow the compilation or the developer should not accept it. Explicit conversion gives predictable results according to the compiler fact sheet.

JERRY WEINBERG
But so does implicit conversion. And, in any case, denoting the type differences that force a conversion changes implicit conversion into explicit conversion. Furthermore, it's not going to create "long declarations in-line" unless there is a conversion demanded by some difference in the declarations. If the programmer doesn't like these, he or she can then change that line to make an explicit conversion of his or her choice, or change the declarations to get a better match. I personally would like the compiler to handle those conversions that are straightforward, and to let me and following readers know that it's done so.

JOSEPH HOWARD
Yes, I like the idea as restated, but I consider it an optional hint. If the compiler denotes the type conversions, it is explicit. And yes, the same type means no conversion. Jerry, the reason I like explicit conversion of no-brainer conversions is that over any period of time, the compiler and word-size variances, versions, and platforms (16 to 32 bit, 32 to 64 bit) change. Simple conversions on one compiler become problems on another. For this

reason, I tend to use more user-defined types or to document the presumed type.

But the real problem occurs when porting code from one compiler to another. Some compilers perform conversions using different intermediary types (for temporary storage). This is one reason I want the compiler not to do default conversions. Changing data from type to type is an exceptional situation that should be defined explicitly for portability reasons. One compiler's intermediary may be float (double); a second may use float (quad); and a third may use intermediaries of the final (receiving) type and then multiply. Different compilers return different conversions, even with the same word sizes. Explicitly defined intermediaries provide better direct control of the converted types.

JERRY WEINBERG
Yes, without a standardization among compilers that reaches the proper level of detail, there is always a danger when porting. In other words, the underlying stupid trick here is depending on the compiler to be consistent across environments.

There is always a danger in having too many conversions when porting, even if they're explicit, because the compilers are different—and so, perhaps, are the computers. I'd say that ports require explicit examination and testing of each conversion, and that the fewer conversions you have, the better, by any method. Perhaps a large number of conversions is a critique of our design, and poor designs generally don't port well.

Not Imposing Controls Over the Installation Process

DAVE KLEIST
Another favorite stupid programmer trick: writing non-Y2K compliant code in 1998. Yes, it was in production because at this client, there were no controls over the installation process. (Multiple platforms, too.)

Jerry Weinberg

This was pretty stupid, all right! The real stupidity was not having controls over the installation process, with or without multiple platforms. There are more worms in this can than Y2K, but I know many managers who thought that when the millennium arrived, these problems would cease to exist. Two-digit dates may not be portable across centuries, but stupidity certainly has proved to be.

Lessons

Jerry Weinberg and James Bullock

All of the tricks in this chapter are about dependencies: creating dependencies on specific implementation details and noting dependencies when we encounter them. Once we realize that all code will be ported—to another release, compiler, or platform—it is clear that dependencies have to be managed. What destroys portability is having dependencies you can't find.

1. Put a big red flag around the dependent procedures—explain what each does, and when the code is ported, rewrite those parts.
2. Don't build things that depend on implementation details, in the first place: data structures, implementation details, messages, and so on.
3. Optimization depends on implementation details (of the hardware and software), so don't do it unless you have to. Optimize last, and only where you really need it.
4. Identify types and conversions explicitly.

3

Stupid Design Tricks

> **The Thread**
>
> *Now the discussion turns to tricks we use during design (or instead of design).*
>
> *—Jerry Weinberg*

Failing to Design Your Program Before You Code It

Daniel Starr
I think a real clever programmer trick is this: Design your program before you code it.

Jerry Weinberg
Dan, what are you, some kind of radical fanatic?

Daniel Starr
This is easy to say, but seems to be hard in practice. I see rather few people in the software business who actually design. They draw a few pictures and write a few documents, but this is not design. Design, for me, is the step where you actually go from problem to solution. I think there's a reason for this: Programming attracts many technologists and few designers.

So, what passes for design in many programming projects seems to be more like high-level coding. There are some tools for this—higher-level languages, compilable specifications, and architecture description languages, for instance. The trouble I see is that there is still this step between problem and solution in which one creates the representation of each and assures that the solution really solves the problem. You can't do this just by raising the level of the language for describing one or the other; you have to do a real creative act in the middle.

Of course, since design is often an invisible act, and there aren't many in the business who do it all that well (or are all that interested in it, since it involves few nifty tools and toys), it's easy to shortchange design in our project management. Sure, we'll allow some time for design—just long enough to write a document that nobody will read, or to write some very high-level code-like *stuff* that we can then refine into real code.

So, that's my clever programmer trick. And now I'll suggest one that's even cleverer: Architect your system before you design it and before you code it.

But this makes "programming" look mighty insignificant. . . .

Jerry Weinberg

Now you've really gone off the deep end! Why, the next thing you'll be doing is bringing up that building analogy again, and saying that we should architect and design our buildings before we start laying bricks. Who ever heard of such a thing?

Dwayne Phillips

I must chime in with Mr. Starr. In the past eighteen months, I have helped with six software projects. Design happened in only one of them (performed by an SEI Level 3 organization).

I started programming in 1978. I did not learn how to design programs and how to design them before coding until 1995. I think I am typical.

I have visited software projects in which the team lead has fifteen years of software and the team members have five-to-ten years of experience. They know what they are doing! If you don't believe it, just ask their management.

But they don't know how to design. And since everyone knows how experienced the team is, I cannot convince anyone that these people don't know how to design and don't do any design.

In one of these organizations, we have major design reviews. The projects are about two-thirds software and one-third custom hardware. The hardware engineers stand up and brief their designs with wonderful graphics. They discuss how they ran simulations on the air flow through the hardware, temperature hot spots, form factors, and so on. You can see that they created three or four designs and evaluated them against project goals to pick the best one.

The software guys stand up and show a flow chart that took fifteen minutes to draw, calling it their design. It is embarrassing to be associated with software, sometimes.

Question: How do you explain to someone that the software team has not done any design?

Failing to Consider at Least Three Design Alternatives

JERRY WEINBERG
One absolutely minimal test is the Rule of Three, as you saw practiced by the hardware engineers:

> *If you haven't evaluated at least three alternative designs, you haven't designed.*

Your software people wouldn't pass that simple test, but do your managers know enough to believe that?

DWAYNE PHILLIPS
No, my managers don't know enough to believe that. Any tips on how to teach them or, better yet, how to get them to teach themselves?

JERRY WEINBERG
That's a crisp challenge. I do this all the time, face-to-face, with some success (and some failure, too). It usually takes some time, so I don't know if I can easily write a short script. (You could tell them, "Jerry Weinberg says so!" but if they believe it because of that, who knows what fool they'll listen to next.)

I suspect that I can't answer easily because the question always surprises me. I think, "How can anyone not know that?" But, of course, few seem to. I guess I have a little trouble with the reality of such ignorance.

Making It Overly Complex

BRIAN GULINO
Constants upset me.

Earlier, Sue Petersen mentioned a payroll example in which a special case became two special cases and was hard-coded into the payroll routine, something like this:

```
if idEmployee = "bigcheese" then do
        *special processing
end
```

The routine needed to be changed to this:

```
if idEmployee = "bigcheese" or idEmployee = "specialguy" then do
      *special processing
end
```

A test run with four employees—the two "magic" ones and two controls—would adequately test this and you're done in less than an hour.

Consider what would happen if a good programmer wrote it:

```
read exceptionlist from control file
        loop through exceptionlist searching for idEmployee
if found then do special processing
```

To add the second employee, you have to

1. Find the control file.
2. Make sure the control file you find is the one used by the program when its path and environment variables are set up (there are probably two or more on the system with the same name).
3. Figure out the syntax of the control file and add the second employee ID.

The test run must make sure that your guess on the correct control file was right. Personally, I'm never quite sure of this until the code actually gets into production. Elapsed time: a lot more than an hour.

A truly professional programmer would write this:

```
*/include dialect specific api
if idEmployee =
    apicall0014(idHunt,idType,fileControl,callType,machineType)
```

To add the second employee:

1. Download API documentation from the Web.
2. Examine include for meaning of five parameters passed to apicall11014.
3. Examine documentation for how to modify for adding another employee.
4. Modify API call—get cryptic error message.
5. Develop work around for API bug and install enhancement.

Elapsed time: still more than an hour. Is there some sort of guild that says we have to work like this?

Jerry Weinberg
Not if you don't add employees! No wonder people think computers aren't flexible.

I think there's a design problem here, based on the need to have a special compensation routine for one employee. Why not have one separate entry point where you come in with gross pay, for those who don't follow the ordinary patterns? It would seem easier to do gross pay by hand, especially since the compensation plan is likely to change soon.

How come we call it *soft*ware, anyway?

Designing Without Thinking

Dave Kleist
To me, design is like thought, and design documentation like language. You need both to express yourself, your intentions, and so on, but you can have one without the other (for example, aphasia, or Koko the gorilla, arguably).

Jerry Weinberg
I think Koko is a chimp. I could be wrong, though.

Dave Kleist

I believe it is possible to have good designs (like good thoughts) without having expressed them in design documentation. I can point to real-world items that I believe have solid designs without a lick of documentation. A few would be: the human body, the ecosphere of Earth, and the universe. (I don't think that religious texts supply enough information to be considered design documentation; executive summaries, maybe.)

Jerry Weinberg

And, indeed, most real systems we deal with are mostly designed indigenously, with no documents whatsoever—like the system we have for getting along with our neighbors, or, indeed, the irrigation system around here, where I live in New Mexico. It has lasted more than 300 years (and wasn't affected by Y2K at all).

Dave Kleist

Lest anyone misinterpret my position: I like artifacts. In my experience, however, the much larger problem is that people don't know how to design (that is, to think). Coaching people into thinking is harder than telling them to produce document *X*, so focusing on design usually turns into "Write up one of these." I've read too many 200-page documents that were completely useless, and I've gotten too many yeses when I've asked (literally), "Am I the only one who sees problems with this?"

Jerry Weinberg

Dave, I really like the clarity of your comment. It makes me think that the really good designs are always under-documented. They surprise us by responding well to situations we had no logical right to believe they would handle. For instance, the design is not just what's there, but what's not there—and what's not there is potentially infinite. To be more specific, many well-designed programs simply did not have Y2K problems, but you're unlikely to read in their documents anything about Y2K.

Missing the Key Driver of Risk

JAMES BULLOCK

Here's my favorite stupid programmer trick (meaning, the way I prefer to foul things up): picking the wrong basic model. User scenario design, for a state-heavy system; communicating sequential processes to implement a simple browse and update.

There's a related dumb project trick that sometimes applies to the system, but also applies to other aspects of the project: missing the key driver of risk. Missing the one thing that is most different, unique, or challenging about the system. Here are some examples of risk drivers that are often overlooked:

- Building high-volume embedded controls, parts cost matters immensely. So, code size matters immensely. Optimizations for speed don't matter a whole lot when controlling room or house temperature.
- Building a very large tactical system, the sheer size of the code base is the largest issue. The process dynamics for handling things, for example the throughput of the change review board, dominated the project risks.
- Building ERP systems, I'm learning that the dominating issue is project integration, not system integration. It dominates all the other concerns, of which there are several.

Being Penny-Wise and Pound-Foolish on Moral Grounds

JERRY WEINBERG

I recall a company with more than fifty thousand employees, four of whom were for some reason given a special payment each period for garaging their cars. This special case was causing no end of trouble, until I pointed out that maintaining this code was costing more than the actual garage payments. We figured out that it would be cheaper and easier to pay them with a manual cash voucher once a year, so we did—though not without opposition. One bean-counter type argued that if we paid them once at the beginning of the year, they would get away with extra money if they happened to quit before the year was over. He couldn't stand the idea that it was cheaper to give them an extra hundred bucks than to do the "moral" thing.

So, stupid programmer tricks don't always come from programmers; sometimes, the stupid thing is writing code rather than arguing with stupid customers.

Another time, the State Treasurer of one of the Southwestern states refused to accept a program that tallied all the state's bond payments once a month—because the cross-footed totals were sometimes off by a penny because of rounding. Mathematically, this difference could not be prevented "honestly," and the Treasurer insisted that we could not fudge the penny into one bond or another—even though we were talking about billions of dollars.

Since we couldn't do it honestly and we couldn't do it dishonestly, there was no way the program could do it. I offered the Treasurer five dollars out of my own pocket, enough to cover the discrepancy for a few hundred years, but all I got for my efforts was a morally indignant dismissal from the project.

So, this stupid programming trick is the old penny-wise and pound-foolish paradox, based on some irrelevant idea of morality. And, I have no idea whatsoever about what we can do to prevent it.

Failing to Think in Terms of Trade-Offs

SUE PETERSEN

Regarding the comments earlier, on system-assigned keys: Sometimes, we do this because the existing facility isn't flexible enough. My system does have a routine to assign an arbitrary key, but the assignment happens just before the record is added to the database. This makes it hard to use the field to link Master-Detail records. Sure, I could "do it right" and code around it. But doing so is a lot more complex than creating my own arbitrary key. And I have a simple mind!

Coding, or *any* type of programming, for that matter, is a matter of making intelligent trade-offs. It's easy to sit back and criticize the choices someone else makes, and there are times when I really do enjoy a rousing debate about arbitrary keys versus intelligent keys in a database. But I think this is missing the point. It's usually a lot more important for the coder to *think* about the choices she's making than to make the politically correct choice. And we should all realize that the correct choice may change in the future as the world changes under our feet. As Jerry pointed out earlier, playing games with date fields in some systems might even have been sensible . . . forty years ago.

War stories are fun, and I still chortle every time I think about Daniel Starr's DEATHSTARR coder. But I'd sure like to know more about how to make intelligent trade-offs in the field.

JERRY WEINBERG
It starts with the realization that you are making trade-offs and that there's no way around it, except to shut off your brain.

Binding Too Early or Too Late

SHARON MARSH ROBERTS
Here's a stupid analyst trick and a stupid programmer trick all rolled into one.

The problem is defining fields flexibly. Many financial products and programs have rates and amounts expressed as specific fields. And as any math-savvy person knows, you can add, subtract, multiply, and divide those particular fields.

However, you can't if someone bastardizes the field. The most memorable situation I can remember was the advent of variable-rate mortgages. Suddenly, a once-stable rate (12 percent, 5 percent, 3 percent, and 7.5 percent) could be set to change during the term of the mortgage. Well, there would have been plenty of work in just implementing the fix to have the system calculate the APR and create the appropriate mortgage disclosure documents. But someone devised a stupid trick to make the process easier: Instead of changing the screen to accept an added value, *V* for variable rates or *F* for fixed rates, he threw the *V* into the rate field itself.

A second example is a database design of an HR system in which the designer gave the employee entity an attribute of "attribute" (and had a corresponding "attribute type" to help define it).

Why was this stupid? Because nobody could figure out how to use such flexibility without making normal systems behavior and performance impossible.

In the first example, the problem arose when normal calculations were performed across loans. The computer performed necessary transformations, at which point most calculations were either infinite or meaningless. Or both. With the field corrupted by *V*, you would never be able to automatically calculate the average rate across mortgages again. Except in Excel or manually.

In the second example, the number of joins performed to find out whether an employee was male or female, or in what division the person was assigned, was about three, rather than a standard single-table query. The number of joins required to find out whether the employee's record had the required attributes was just too many for the system to handle. It froze dead on execution.

Why do people do tricks like these? They're getting out of programming or thinking "right now." If you're afraid to think about the problem, the solution you design will be suboptimal at best.

JERRY WEINBERG

This is definitely the dark twin to the problem of constants—binding too late versus binding too early. I guess the extreme of late binding would be to have the user write the program at the moment of use—which I think shows the trap in binding too late. Choosing when to bind which values is, as you say, an analyst job, and one that cannot be deferred. Or perhaps you could have meta-binding, where the analyst decides to let the user enter a "binding time" for each application, or each use of each application. But, then, we could have meta-meta-binding, where you let the user decide when to bind the binding time.

Sharon Marsh Roberts
I find that such tricks also occur in general ledger account code creation.

Accounting package vendors are tempted to try to make fields multipurpose, which often means that they're unfit for any particular purpose and are manipulated correctly only by the knowledgeable folk who built or maintain the system.

So much for using database theory in databases!

This trick can be prevented by first analyzing the problem and potential solution set carefully; second, programming carefully; and third, by not trying to be too abstract or clever.

In other words, there is no certain substitute for intelligent effort.

Jerry Weinberg
Darn! Why do we keep coming back to that? Why can't we just do stupid things and get intelligent results?

Sharon Marsh Roberts
Oh, what a tangled web we weave when first we practice to not practice.

Writing a Program When No Program Is Needed

Jerry Weinberg
One of the biggest stupid design tricks is writing a program when no program is needed.

In our introductory programming courses, we always gave at least one assignment in which the solution could be obtained in less than five minutes using pencil and paper. We never said "program a solution", we always said "solve this problem." But we knew that in a programming course, most students would *assume* that we wanted a program, not a solution. Anybody who did that flunked the assignment (which meant they had to do it over to pass). We wanted them to remember this lesson, always.

Camus once said, "Seek your advisor, seek your advice." If you bring a problem to a programmer, you'll get a program. If you bring your problem to a problem-solver, you'll get a solution, which may or may not be a program. I prefer working with problem-solvers.

Lessons

JAMES BULLOCK

All of these design tricks are about remembering to do design. It is far too tempting, with a problem in hand, to leap directly to a solution and start building. The open-ended exploration of alternatives often looks like nothing is happening, but it can lead to far more powerful solutions than "just do it."

1. Honor the creative act of connecting a solution to a problem, and checking that it actually solves the problem.
2. Apply the Rule of Three. If you haven't evaluated at least three alternative designs, you haven't designed.
3. Ask, "Does the design really have to cover this case?" Leave out stuff that costs more than it is worth.
4. Coach people into thinking, don't just force them into writing big documents.
5. Watch for, and encourage, good designs—the ones that surprise us by responding well to situations we had no "right" to believe they would handle.
6. Pick the right basic model. Don't use scenario design for a state-heavy system, or communicating sequential processes for a simple browse and update.
7. Pick the right time to bind values, definitions, and structure. Sometimes sooner is better, sometimes later is better.

4

Stupid Design Document Tricks

The Thread

Stupid tricks are not limited to programming and design. No, there are also many tricks for using (and abusing) documentation.

—Jerry Weinberg

Leaving No Design Artifacts and No Garbage

JOSEPH HOWARD
Evidence of design is in the artifacts of the project; where there are no artifacts, there is no design. (No state diagrams, no entity definitions, no attribute definitions, and so forth, means no design and no analysis.)

JERRY WEINBERG
But Joseph, some of my clients tell me that the code contains the design (and the analysis, and the problem statement, and so on).

JOSEPH HOWARD
It's like archaeology, where no garbage dumps means no people lived there. A small amount of trash means a short-term visit.

JERRY WEINBERG
I like to see projects save their trash, but although online development ought to make that easy, it's generally used to erase the entire garbage trail. Losing your garbage is a stupid programmer trick since it erases your data for learning.

DAVE KLEIST
But it's a devious bad-manager trick (no documentation, no proof).

JAMES BULLOCK
No proof. Seems to betray a bit of insecurity about the system produced.

Daniel Starr

Jerry mentioned that losing your garbage is a stupid programmer trick, since it erases your data for learning.

Is this why, when you visit the office of a really good programmer or designer, you find so much paper? I know I still have ten- and fifteen-year-old documents, the garbage of design and development efforts, and I still find useful things in them.

When I started at Bell Labs, we had this wonderful mechanism called the "memorandum for file" (MF). You'd be working on something, whatever it was, and when you reached an important point that needed to be reported, you'd write an MF (ignore the other possible meanings of this abbreviation). The MFs all went into an enormous company file, with some indexing by keyword but also an online listing through the company library by date, title, and author. It was a great way to preserve some of the debris produced by design.

Jerry Weinberg

MFs can be grossly misused—as when the writer is trying to put an "I-told-you-so" paper trail where it can be pulled out in self-defense when the project fails (or forgotten if the project succeeds). These are CYA (cover your anterior) memos. What we want are CYA (consider your alternatives) memos, to show what things we thought of but then thought better of.

Daniel Starr

Needless to say, we no longer do this. I haven't written an MF in years, and don't know if the service even exists. When documents went online, and now to the intranet, these files disappeared. Ten years from now, we'll still be able to tell why we did some of the things we did in the early days of our current systems, but the trail disappears in the early 1990's. Unless, of course, we decide to recycle all those old, "worthless" memos (and we might—remember, once upon a time Warner Bros. dumped all their old Looney Tunes animation cells into a landfill, thinking that old cartoons had no value).

Mistaking Documents for Documentation

DAVE KLEIST
I don't consider a design to be a document: An artifact is a reflection of the design. Design, to me, is an artificial construct and process that can only be recorded through documentation, but it isn't the documentation itself. Confusing the two is one big reason why many projects still fail while containing reams of documentation (this goes for analysis and anything else).

JERRY WEINBERG
Such projects don't have reams of documentation; they have reams of *documents*. They're not the same, which is what I think you're saying by calling them artifacts. I find it helps to keep these two words straight—one of the best ways of documenting a design (or a process) is to videotape an interview with the designer(s).

DAVE KLEIST
You're back into cargo cult programming if you only produce artifacts. An artifact is not proof that any intelligent thought has gone into the process. You can have a system built on a solid design that some brilliant soul kept locked in his or her head, and a worthless morass of programs that have every aspect documented.

JERRY WEINBERG
But don't ignore the problem of the brilliant, but locked, head. It's rather difficult to review designs that are documented that way, just as it's difficult (in other words, impossible) to review designs that are documented in reams of documents. A design's documentation ought to be simpler to understand (at its level) than the system itself; otherwise, why have a design at all? That's another check on designing.

JAMES BULLOCK
I'm wondering if there is a model here around "aboutness." All the pointless documents are *about* the design (or analysis, or whatever), but not *on point:* not the actual thing itself, not even meaningful commentary on the thing itself. This is the basis

for many objections to methodologies, standards, and templates: They allow aboutness. Big binders with "everything" done right, except grappling with the actual issues at hand.

I know when people are talking, writing, meeting, and directing around the issue. It's a stupid trick at any level, and in any context.

JERRY WEINBERG
It's the difference between knowing something and knowing about something. Sometimes I ask, "What do you know?" Sometimes that short-circuits these around-about meetings.

Coding from the Wrong Type of Document

DANIEL STARR
One of the things I learned while working in the communications software industry (telephone switching and related stuff, in particular) is that one of the ways you can divide problems into two big classes is this:

- Sometimes the solution looks like what the user does with the system.
- Sometimes it doesn't.

Some systems can be coded from use cases, scenarios, or other models of the users' interactions with the data in the system. A simple case is control of an automated teller machine (ATM). The design of the software pretty much falls out of the description of the interactions between the user and the ATM.

Some systems, by the nature of the problem, can't be made this way without all kinds of problems. Telephone call processing is one such problem. While the specifications for features are written in the form of scenarios describing the interactions between users and the telephone system, woe to anyone who tries to code these scenarios to implement the actual features! I know from sad experience the kind of mess you can get into by doing this. The features interact; you can invoke one feature from the middle of another; some combinations of features are nonsensical (but you have to be able to recognize the nonsense). The software for call processing has to take a form that is sort of a level above the scenarios themselves—it has to be a "machine for creating call scenarios." This is a tough design problem, and there is no doubt in my mind that the design for a good call processing system does not simply fall out of the analysis of the problem.

Of course, when the design does fall out of the problem analysis (which it does for a lot of the administrative stuff that goes on in a telephone system), the designers need to be smart enough to recognize this fact and not get overly cute. A long, long time ago, I didn't recognize this and built a very clever, table-driven system for doing recent changes (basically a database application—a set of predefined transactions with consistency and sanity checks). It would have been simpler and more maintainable just to code the small number of (noninteracting) scenarios.

JAMES BULLOCK
Dan's description of two kinds of systems reminds me of the one about the two kinds of people in the world: Those who divide people into two kinds, and those who don't.

JERRY WEINBERG
Did you hear the one about the three kinds of people in the world? Those who can count, and those who can't.

Mistaking Documents for the Design

DANIEL STARR
In our architecture review process, we review architectures—problems and solutions, not documents. We tell people this in advance. You can give us documents, but we will not promise to read them (some reviewers like to read documents and come prepared with questions; others, like me, show up cold and respond strictly to what they see).

JERRY WEINBERG
Or hear. I know you respond to what you hear, and even more often to what you smell.

DANIEL STARR

The review is an oral exam, so if the design only exists in the head of one brilliant designer, then that designer had better be at the review to explain it to our team. And while you're at it, you might want to have some of the project members sit in and watch. We have had reviews double as tutorials; we add some special ground rules about interaction between the presenters and the spectators, and it seems to work. I haven't had project members ask to videotape a review, but I would have no objection to it, as long as they are making the tape for their own use.

Failing to Design Your Documents

DANIEL STARR

On the subject of documents, good designers design their documents as well as their systems. Documents get created for many purposes, audiences, and dispositions. Here are some examples:

- *To describe the user experience to those who will use the product.* Note that while we often think about writing user manuals after the system is built, developing prototype user manuals early allows us to test the external appearance of the system easily and cheaply. I will go so far as to say that the user manual (or enough of it for users to determine whether or not they like the product) is one of the first things you should create. I did this on one project (twenty years ago), and it really worked—the system described by the predevelopment user manual (and approved by the key users) was very, very close to the final system.
- *To assist in the partitioning and design of the system.* The audience for this kind of document is the design team itself and the reviewers. This kind of document may be more valuable in the writing than in the reading, and there may be no need to maintain it unless it's also trying to accomplish one of the following:

    - to describe to implementors what is actually going to be built (a "blueprint")
    - to describe to future redesigners what actually *was* built (an "as-built blueprint")

- *To break down the work and manage the implementation process.* While this should be maintained as the work breakdown and scheduling evolve, once the project is more or less "done," these documents should be archived rather than maintained.

I think part of the problem with documents is that we mix them up. In particular, we mix document types that are fundamentally temporary, like work breakdowns and blueprints, with documents that should be long-lived, like user experience descriptions and as-built blueprints. The temporary documents tend to be really big, so when we try to make them "living documents," we create huge amounts of work—and a great temptation to view the documentation as irrelevant.

Jerry Weinberg
As you say, it's a design problem; also, designing *is* more difficult when you're trying to do too many interacting things with one system. Very few people want to write two separate documents about what they consider one system, and managers encourage the muddling together of different functions because they believe this will save time and money. Wrong.

Simple for the Programmer; Incomprehensible to the User

Shaper
[At this point, one of the Shapers gave an extended example of a rule-based system to deal with systems of variable codes. The simple example was rather long, and to many Shapers, not simple at all.]

Jerry Weinberg
I'm being devil's advocate here. It can be a stupid programmer trick to define a system with so much flexibility that it cannot

be tested with any level of confidence. For example, tables can simplify structure, and thus make testing easier, but they can also complicate structure by allowing such an enormous (astronomical) number of parameter combinations that testing becomes impossible. We always have to ask, "Do the users really need that much flexibility? Does it buy them more than it will cost us? Will it be easier or harder for them to program than a VCR?"

Shaper

Incorrect flexibility can be a bad thing, but then, Jerry, what are you advocating to replace this trick?

Jerry Weinberg

I think the principle I have in mind is that sometimes, when a complex trick is needed to implement an application, it's the application that's stupid, not the programmer. I remember, years ago, listening to an all-day seminar at IBM about a gloriously complex system that IBM was selling to the Internal Revenue Service. At the end of the seminar, one of the Germans in attendance wasn't impressed. He said, "If you had a sensible tax system, you wouldn't need such a complex system." I've never forgotten that we always need to consider this possibility. As one of the great architects once said, "The architect's first job is to take what's given and change it."

Brian Gulino

This reminds me of some rule-based systems I've created or worked on to edit transactions or to set up financial statements in business applications. Some meta-rules apply:

1. Rule-based systems are difficult to write and document.
2. Assuming success with item 1, rule-based systems are difficult to present to the user in a manner that makes it easy for him to enter the rules. We'll call this user the rule creator. Successful interfaces usually feature well-designed GUIs—there's a lot of complicated stuff going on that can be well represented, visually.

If you succeed with items 1 and 2, you are to be congratulated. Most commercial-grade software packages don't get this right. I do a significant amount of business going into companies following the departure of the CFO. I pore through manuals and code to figure out how to set up rule-based financial statements in what are supposed to be turnkey packages. It's rarely easy, usually time-consuming, and always gets everybody mad. In addition to losing the CFO, these companies have a big programming bill that nobody really wants in the budget.

3. The killer is this item, meta-rule 3, which is the general feeling of disempowerment these rule-based systems give the data entry people. The rule-creator, usually the CFO, creates this thing, but to the data entry people, the system seems to arbitrarily throw out various codes. They master some of the common, obvious rules and don't quite get the more subtle rules—and then the rules change!

The users react as disempowered people do—they approach the system with fear and trepidation. Superstitions develop, complex theories of operation are advanced and discarded, and odd dependencies are postulated and shared.

The rule-creator never sees a problem. He has eliminated all those troublesome mistakes the clerical people used to make. He just has a few more things to work out in the new transaction control module. Now, if only he could do something about the turnover in accounting—but that's out of his control.

JERRY WEINBERG
Thanks, Brian, for describing in detail what I've seen many times, and was trying to warn against.

Thinking "I'll Be Gone By Then"

SHARON MARSH ROBERTS
Let's get down to business on what our options are with respect to the unwieldy structure known as the general ledger account.

Organizations are complex and wonderful things. There is no "one size fits all" model for how to build the hierarchy of an organization. Even if an organization says it is flat, reporting and responsibility still exist on various levels.

One example is the banking subsidiary of a financial services firm in which HR employees are located in each of the operating units. The reporting structure is Company —> Subsidiary —> NY Regional Office —> HR. Because it's a matrix organization, the summarization for HR is Company —> HR —> Subsidiary —> NY Regional Office. Reports exist at each level, with the top two levels being either the company and its subsidiary or the company and HR. Both reporting structures exist, and both need to be acknowledged in the code for an expense.

Some of the more intellectually satisfying packages allow for rules tables, identifiers of account code segments, and breaks between account code segments, which may be required for the rules tables. All three features are necessary in order to construct a ledger that can be understood by a naïve accountant. The final goal is to make accounting reports intelligible or intelligent to the manager who uses these reports to identify and analyze problems. He or she is neither an accountant nor a programmer and has no interest in becoming either.

I don't think that flexibility in itself is wrong, but flexibility can be substituted with careful analysis of the data definitions and of the rules surrounding the functionality. Whether rules are in a table, function as the triggers for a table, or are translated more immediately into code is a question for the technical manager based on how the language (3GL or 4GL) functions. The general rule is to not circumvent whatever is built into the language (thereby forgoing some of the other stupid programmer tricks already mentioned).

Rules do exist. In the above example, the HR tag at the fourth level can only exist in an operating unit. It is translated into an identifier at the second level, in order to allow reporting for all of HR. So, if HR is the fourth-level tag in report structure 1, then the alternate report structure must have an HR in the second level.

There are probably dozens of other rules, such as requiring marketing department expenses to be attached to products, not to other business units. So "MKT" must follow a product designation, not NY Regional Office.

The "bad seed" of account codes is the need to make the function of the account sequence dependent upon some combination that will someday collapse under its own weight. For example, let's assume the third accounting code segment is either the product, the overhead organization, or the country (to identify the foreign parts of our business). Our risk is that someday, we will need to know which product was sold in which foreign country and we'll discover that we have no mechanism to specify both.

What's the underlying stupid analysis there? It's believing that we'll never have enough business outside the U.S. to need that combination. It's thinking that we won't be using this particular package long enough for that problem to arise. (Twenty-five years is not an unusual life span for a general ledger package in a company.)

JERRY WEINBERG

The account code discrepancy and its relation to organization structure is a cousin of the Y2K problem, which is part of the general class called the "I'll be gone by then" problem. The fact is that documents carry only a small part of the documentation of a design. Whatever documentation scheme we use, the fundamental source of information about a design is the person who created that design. Where that person goes, most of our information goes, and our users may be left with an unusable product.

Lessons

JERRY WEINBERG

There are designs, design documentation, and design documents. These are three different things, and many stupid tricks result from imagining that one is the other.

1. Documenting the process of designing is at least as useful as documenting the end design.
2. Design and design process documentation are about CYA—consider your alternatives (not the other CYA).
3. Useful records of design include the thing itself or meaningful commentary on the thing itself, not about and around the thing.
4. Review the architecture or the design, not the documents.
5. Design the user experience of any document you produce.
6. Design for the right problem. An intractable design is a signal that the problem, or at least the problem as stated, may be wrong.

5

Tricks Arising from Social Inadequacy

The Thread

Stupid tricks have even been developed for dealing with (or avoiding) interaction with others.
—Jerry Weinberg

Career Development Through Co-Dependency

DAVE KLEIST
Another stupid trick is career development through co-dependency. It is the learned helplessness in which all independent action is tossed out in favor of latching onto a coworker and coercing him or her into solving all the problems. The co-dependent person completes an assignment at the expense of the coworker. (I've found it's a dance that I have to let finish, once the song is over. Cutting in only extends the whole mess, for both parties.)

JERRY WEINBERG
And for you, too. You become co-co-dependent.

Using Technical Tricks to Avoid Social Situations

FRITZ
My favorite stupid programmer trick is solving a problem I feel competent to solve rather than the one that most needs solving. (Usually, the first is a technical problem and the second is a people problem.)

For example, the month before I went to PSL,[1] our e-mail server started failing under load. It quickly became clear that there was a magic number somewhere that we needed to increase, but the folks we were allowed to talk to at our e-mail vendor and our operating system vendor didn't have the information we needed. At that point, the problem wasn't technical any more—it was the social problem of how to reach someone

[1] PSL stands for Problem Solving Leadership, a Weinberg and Weinberg workshop.

who knew which magic number to change. What I spent the most energy on, however, were palliative technical measures. I did a very good job of making the failures annoying rather than disastrous, and a less good job of stopping the failures themselves.

(I finally got a useful response, from a manager at the operating system vendor, by sending a message to the Usenet group com.sys.<vendor>.bugs. I think the bugs may have aroused a natural desire in the manager to defend his system by pointing out our ignorance, in addition to his straightforward desire to be helpful.)

This is my favorite flavor of stupidity because it's so easy to overlook—after all, the technical problem does get solved. So, part of preventing the stupidity is simply becoming aware of it: The postmortem I wrote just before going to PSL didn't frame the issue in terms of technical versus social issues at all, though that seems obvious to my post-PSL self. The other (harder?) part is acting on the fact that I don't always have the luxury of sticking to the things I do best.

JERRY WEINBERG

Actually, the luxury is getting to do things that you don't do well. That's the only way to learn wholly new things, but other people (also) want us to keep doing the things we do well (for them). That's how we become experts—and get stuck in our expertise.

Not Documenting Your Assumptions

PAT FERDINANDI

I think we can expand this from programming to other areas of software development. One trick I try not to do but fall into often is . . . making assumptions!

JERRY WEINBERG

Right, but I wish somebody would tell me just how to stop making assumptions. And, by the way, no need to apologize for stretching the thread—assuming is a stupid programmer trick, too. One of the finest, though not one of the rarest. It's often another case of trying to avoid an uncomfortable or inconvenient social situation. Just assume the answers, then you don't have to talk to anyone!

PAT FERDINANDI
You can't stop *making* assumptions. Nor should you; assuming is sometimes an appropriate strategy. If it's going to take weeks or months to find out for sure what the requirement is, and you're pretty sure (with greater than 75 percent probability in your estimate) that the requirement will turn out to be *X* rather than *Y*, it makes sense to assume that the requirement is indeed *X*. You can't just stop at making the assumption—you need to document, in a place where you'll find it, the fact that *X* is an assumption rather than a requirement, how far into actual development you can go before *X* becomes irreversible, and your plan for verifying that *X* is indeed the requirement.

Assumptions are tools (like knives) and can be used for good or ill. Programming is a craft (or so said Brooks, and I think he's right), and good craftspeople know the capabilities, limitations, and safe uses of their tools.

JERRY WEINBERG
All right, I agree—as far as this goes. But I thought (assumed) the assumptions Pat was talking about were the ones that we don't realize we're making. Those are the kind I don't know how to stop making, or even become aware of, so that I can document or clarify them as necessary. So, I still need help with this.

Not Asking for Help

DANIEL STARR
Jerry, you said the secret word—"help." (Watch out for falling ducks!) You can't find all your own assumptions, and the ones you don't know you're making are the ones that bite you.

So, ask for help. Have your designs, concepts, and problem definitions reviewed by independent people. Sometimes all you have to do is tell them what you're planning to do, and watch their facial expressions. If they get confused, it may be because you're assuming something and they don't get it.

Jerry Weinberg
I guess this is the stupidest programmer or analyst trick of all: not asking for help. Nobody is smart enough to do this business alone.

James Bullock
The answer to Jerry's question about reacting to invisible assumptions is to make them visible. Doing proofs in math is good practice, I think. My college math sequence involved "proving calculus," starting with a couple of set axioms. Toward the end, I got tripped up less often on thinking I knew things I didn't really know. Unfortunately, unless you've got the time to ask yourself, "Do I really know that?" for four or five hours straight, once a week, for two years, I can't help you with surfacing assumptions.

Jerry Weinberg
This reminds me of the "Do You Mean?" game, which is definitely a way to uncover assumptions. One person makes a statement about the situation that they believe to be true. The other person replies with a question starting "Do you mean . . . ?" You can't move to the next supposedly true statement until you get *N* (usually three) *yes* answers in a row. Get a friend and try it out.

Preventing Others from Learning, by Being Impatient

Dave Smith
Of the stupid things I do with some regularity, one of the worst may be indulging my impatience and pushing ahead with my solution, thereby robbing team members of the chance to think something through themselves and possibly to offer up better suggestions.

Looking back on things I regret, many have to do with missed opportunities to let people learn.

Jerry Weinberg
It's always hard for me to think of myself as an impediment to someone's learning. I try not to do this on the SHAPE forum,

but I'm afraid I often fail. Still, it's also a stupid trick not to forgive yourself for being human—and perhaps enthusiastic rather than simply impatient.

Failing to Notice Your Fault Feedback Ratio and to Do Something About It

JERRY WEINBERG
This item just came in over the Internet:

> *PROGRAMMER'S DRINKING SONG*
> *100 little bugs in the code,*
> *100 bugs in the code,*
> *fix one bug, compile it again, 101 little bugs in the code.*
> *101 little bugs in the code . . .*
> *Repeat until BUGS = 0*

This is certainly one of the stupidest programmer tricks—not noticing that you're putting in more bugs than you're taking out, or, as we say, the Fault Feedback Ratio (FFR) is greater than one.[2] How to combat it? One way is to record, with each new line of code, the time and date that the code went into the source code database, and the number of the bug that prompted the code's insertion (if any). Then you can get a handle on lines of code that were put in to fix other lines of code—not a perfect match to FFR, but a start at awareness. Any other ideas?

Not Documenting Why Choices Were Made

JESSE GORDON
I don't have any contributions about the FFR question, but the technique mentioned partially corrects a stupid programmer trick (SPT)—that of not documenting code properly. For me, not documenting properly means not including explanations of why certain coding choices or constructs were used, as well as not properly cross-referencing code for defect fixes (by at least

---

2 For more on the Fault Feedback Ratio, see Gerald M. Weinberg, *Quality Software Management, Vol. 2: First-Order Measurement* (New York: Dorset House Publishing, 1993), p. 242.

indicating on the added or changed lines which defect fix they were dropped for).

The result of this SPT is code that is more difficult to understand, maintain, and apply new fixes to. I ran into this recently on a major project. I do software performance analysis, so I often need to change code. But before I do, I want to understand why the code is as it is, so I can understand the ramifications of the proposed changes. This is why I find poorly documented code so infuriating.

What can be done to prevent it? Several things, but most helpful would be documentation that explains the rationale for design choices that are reflected in the code. Jerry's suggestion above would also help. This has also been a problem in the code I have been working with, as few developers cross-reference code changes with defect numbers. This forces me to do version differences after extracting the different levels of the particular module from the code control tool. Developers should also explain problems and solutions in the defect records in the code control tool.

The basic assumption must be that while one person or a small number of people will fix the code, a larger number of people will need to read it and work with it afterward; so, a bit more clarity (and effort) on the part of the one person will save each of the others more work. Note that this extra effort can pay off even if it's your own code and no one else will look at it. When the far-off day comes that you have to modify your old code, you'll be glad you documented it properly.

Lack of Feedback Doesn't Necessarily Mean the Code Was Good

JERRY WEINBERG

This is a nice segue into the addition of truly clever programming tricks. Just as not asking for help is the stupidest programmer trick, I think the cleverest programmer trick is knowing that you're not that smart and encouraging others to look over your code and give you feedback. If you do what Jesse says, you've made it easier for people to examine your code and make sensible remarks after a reasonable period of study.

One of the truly stupid programmer tricks is to interpret lack of feedback on poorly documented code as confirmation that there's nothing wrong with the code. In fact, the proper interpretation is that the code is so sloppy that nobody cares to take the trouble to give you feedback, good or bad. That's like nobody telling you that you need a new mouthwash.

Let Your Tools Do Their Work

PAT MCGEE

Jesse, are you suggesting that developers write comments on each line in the source code with the defect number? That's not what I understood Jerry to be suggesting. Jerry, did I misunderstand you? What I got out of this was that each change in the source code version manager database (SCCS, RCS, PVCS, or whatever) should have the defect number in the revision comments. If that's the case, I think that proper use of the tool would be to have it do the version differences when you want to see what changed for a specific fix. So, the source code would not contain all the historical changes. Those interested in only the current state would look at the code. Those interested in which changes went with specific fixes would look at the difference output of the version manager tool.

This leads me to articulate what I think is a stupid programmer trick: doing things in the text editor that should be done by the revision control tool.

JERRY WEINBERG

It's only stupid if your managers haven't played a Stupid Manager Trick and not provided a revision control tool (RCT). Without an RCT, the best you can do is use source code—though that definitely has the disadvantages that Pat describes. In general, let your tools do their work.

JESSE GORDON

Well, Pat, in response to your question, I *was* suggesting that developers write comments on each line in the source code with the defect number. But, given your response, I've been thinking some more about this. What I have found tedious is having to work with some module that's new to me and figuring out how the code got to where it is. Now, the source code version manager database I am using (CMVC) does let one see the history of a module, the different versions of the code (all of them extractable), and the differences. So, to get the sequence of changes that went into it requires extracting a series of versions and performing each of the incremental differences. Given the effort required to do that, my reaction has been, "Gee, it would be nice to have all this information available in the source code itself." And that is why I suggested what I did.

At a minimum, the source code should have a list of all defect numbers that resulted in changes to that module, perhaps with a short synopsis. I have worked with source code (assembler, at that) in which every line has comments at the end, indicating which defects have changed that line—and I have not found that to distract from readability. Some of this is an issue of what the source code version tool can do. So, let me amend Jerry's comment: "Without a *proper* revision control tool, the best you can do is use source code." I think that captures the spirit of what I was suggesting.

Pat, thank you for your comments. They have made me think more (and more clearly, hopefully) about this issue.

Keeping in the Stuff That's Corrected by Other Stuff

BRIAN KNOPP

Dave Kleist said, *"I've seen them do it because it's too hard to break apart once they build up a head of steam. They don't do any up-front design, so the monster builds until it's too late. It becomes a snarled mess, like a Kevlar version of the Gordian knot."*

Been there, done that. After my first formal code review (which didn't occur until my programming career was four years old, by the way), the primary criticism that I received was that my functions were too large, and that I needed to spend more time breaking the process down into smaller pieces.

One of the reviewers was very kind about it, saying that he used to do it, too, and that he understood the mind-set. And then he reduced me to tears of laughter when he summarized: "It'll be all right if I just keep typing!" I now have that on a T-shirt, as a reminder to avoid that particular stupid trick.

JERRY WEINBERG

This is the same problem people have when writing prose. They think it's like speaking, where if you say something wrong you can correct it with the next thing out of your mouth—well, not correct it really, but improve it, that is, when you didn't say it perfectly in the first place and then you have a new idea—it's sort of like oil painting rather than water colors, if that helps you understand what I mean, but in case you don't know about painting, you see, with oil colors, you can scrape the paint off if you make a mistake and paint over it (actually, you can't scrape it completely off, because a little of the residue will impregnate the canvas, but almost all will come off and you can paint over it—that is, unless you're painting certain light colors over darker colors that might bleed through, well, not bleed through exactly, but can be seen through the light color and maybe influence its impression a bit—not for all viewers, but for those with . . . blah, blah, blah).

The Delete key is the writer's most important tool; same for software writers.

The most absurd case I remember of this kind was a program (without documentation, of course) that I was trying to decipher. The code was full of switches, twisting the flow around pieces of code that didn't work for certain cases and going to other pieces that had been added to handle the cases the original didn't handle. The crowning touch was a switch that finally turned out to precede another switch to tell the flow whether the second switch was really a switch or was being used as a variable this time through.

If you've done it wrong, take it out and replace it with what's right.

Replacing One Big Mess with an Unending Series of Small Messes

NATE MCNAMARA
Here's a stupid programmer trick I pulled recently.

JERRY WEINBERG
Don't you love it when you catch yourself pulling stupid tricks? For me, it always means a learning opportunity, and that's the most exciting thing there is.

NATE MCNAMARA
It's highly C++ specific. The problem I wanted to solve was allowing multiple threads to share the same output logfile. Without some sort of lock, my log messages would be all jumbled up. The designs I considered were the following:

1(a). The simplest, most explicit way,

```
log.lock();
log.write(...);
log.unlock();
```

1(b). Explicit and exception-safe,

```
const locker_t locker(log);
log.write(...);
```

2. Implicit and prevents deadlock,

```
log.write(...); // locking is inside
```

3(a). Implicit, type-safe, extensible, and streams interface,

```
log << ...;
```

Of course, I had to do version 3.a. It's nontrivial because you can chain <<'s together, like so:

```
log << "X is " << x << std::endl;
```

Each application of << is a separate function call, but I wanted to guarantee that the entire line was automatically transmitted to the log. The trick is to create a temporary object; the temporary will hold the lock for its lifetime, which lasts until the end of the statement.

Unfortunately, it's hard to cause the evaluation of log to create a temporary. It's much easier to use a function return value instead. In other words,

3(b). The apple I ate,

```
log() << ...;
```

My stupidity was not realizing the consequences of taking the easy way out. With solution 3(b), if one writes,

```
foo(log());
```

foo may hold the lock for a long time or even deadlock. Further, it's not obvious from looking at the call. I only discovered this after creating a situation that reduced to the above example and then spending a few hours trying to figure out what was going on.

Now I'm trying to decide whether just to document the pitfall, to find a way to make 3(a) work, or to go with 2, the only completely deadlock-proof solution. (Solution 1 is out because 2 is clearly superior to both versions of 1.) I'm leaning toward 3(a), which is much harder to deadlock than 3(b) (but still possible). I don't like simply documenting my goof, but there are plenty of other fires clamoring for my attention at the moment. The problem with 2 is that it makes it a pain to log messages that incorporate multiple types of data, so the quality of the log will go down. Perhaps compromise is possible, something like this:

4. The best of both worlds?

```
log.write(log_buf() << ...);
```

JERRY WEINBERG

I see one more general moral here, a whole class of stupid programmer tricks. We try to avoid a "mess" like the quality of the log going down, but we fail to consider fully the solution to avoiding the mess.

I think it's a design question. As your solution gets more and more complex (and remember, you were trying to avoid a mess in the first place), there's more and more chance that you'll create a mess that's a lot harder to find and deal with. I call this kind of thing "problem displacement," rather than problem solving, because you push a problem from one place to another, perhaps from one form to another.

I think this particular example was an exception to the general pattern, because more often, people push their mess onto someone else. In this case, you seem to have been concerned about the people who have to deal with the log (perhaps that group includes you), rather than with simplifying your own program. Altruistic and laudable, but as you say, a stupid trick all the same. After all, a corrupted log wouldn't make their life easier, would it?

Give a Fresh Start When Needed

Jerry Weinberg

Let me take a moment to tie together the previous two sections. Revision control tools tend to have a built-in assumption that code is developed by small revisions from initially almost-correct code. If there are massive revisions and revisions of revisions, there comes a time when you really want to junk the code and start over.

When you do that, start the RCT over, too. Yes, we want to give maintainers history, as Jesse suggests, but don't burden them with the *prehistory* of false starts. Do them a favor and erase it.

Failing to Use Your Own Product

James Bullock

I like the idea of a "compiler" that provides multiple representations of the source, depending on what you are doing. Isn't it strange how with all these high-end integrated development environments floating around, so little of this kind of "Poor Schmuck Support" exists? Solving the need by dragging information around in multiple places doesn't sit well with me. Humans are the most common perpetrators of update anomalies: Why take the chance?

I wonder how much the tendency to make functions, modules, methods, and so on (pick your jargon) too big is simply because we make it hard to deal with them. Fewer code things means less overhead, so we lump a bunch of work together.

Jerry Weinberg

I think a big part of this problem is the way compiler developers are often cut off from the world of their users. Sure, they use compilers themselves, but their usage is not generally typical of the larger pool of users. And, sadly, lots of compiler writers don't use the tools they so eagerly sell to others.

The same observation applies for numerous software tool developers. They often consider it a matter of hierarchical status that they don't use the "baby tools" that their customers use, and *that* is a truly stupid programmer trick. Doing it is bad enough, but bragging about it is utterly stupid.

Lessons

Jerry Weinberg

It seems we've uncovered another class of stupid programmer tricks: those designed to avoid human interaction. Here are some ways to help yourself out of this problem:

1. Determine if it is a technical problem or a people problem.
2. One way to learn wholly new things is getting to do things that you don't do well.
3. Ask for help from someone else (and see item 4).
4. Know that you're not that smart, so do things to encourage others to look over your code and give you feedback.
5. Always remember that human interaction may take place in the future, perhaps when you aren't even there.

And, of course, there are still our technical issues to be concerned with:

1. Measure the Fault Feedback Ratio.
2. If you've done it wrong, take it out and replace it with what's right.
3. Include explanations of why certain coding choices or constructs were used, and cross-reference code for defect fixes (by at least indicating on the added or changed lines which defect fix they were dropped for).
4. The Delete key is the writer's most important tool; same for software writers.

6

Experts and Gurus as Leaders

The Thread

Here's a topic:

- *What is an expert?*
- *Are there degrees or levels of experts?*
- *If so, how do you define them?*

My two cents: An expert knows when to bend the rules and the consequences for doing so. However, I think there are degrees of experts. The finer breakout includes these groups:

1. *Follower*
2. *Disciple*
3. *Guru*

I guess there are two questions at the root of this topic:

- *What makes someone a guru?*
- *Is that different from an expert?*

—Pat Ferdinandi

"Guru" As a Degrading Term

DWAYNE PHILLIPS

I work for the U.S. Department of Defense. Please frame my comments in that context.

Where I work, I am always referred to as "the software guru." Sometimes this is flattering; many times, it is not. A wise old man (the software guru of a previous job) once remarked that where he came from, in the hills of western Virginia, "guru" was an insult. For some reason, that is something that has stuck in my mind and won't go away.

I don't like the term "guru," partly because of my old friend's comment, and partly because it implies some sort of mystical power. The software guru has presumably sat on a mountain and absorbed knowledge about who should do what and when in a software project. People where I work are a bit frightened by that sort of thing.

Anyway, I acquired my knowledge of software via much more perspiration than absorption.

Being a guru is much more than knowledge and experience. People do software and people will look to someone who has a sense of calm, confidence, peace, and whatever else might set them apart. The guru can talk with people on their level and through questions, stories, jokes, and so on, raise their level.

Maybe I prefer the term software "counselor." A counselor can understand the subject and the people and help them reach higher understanding.

Has anyone else felt funny about the term, "guru"? Can anyone else suggest an alternate term?

JERRY WEINBERG

I've felt funny—actually, stereotyped, degraded, discounted, and misunderstood—about being called guru ever since the first time that term was applied to me. But, then, I feel that way about most labels.

People use labels to arrest thinking and understanding. If you call me "guru," it's not much different from calling me "crazy"—you don't have to think about me anymore. You don't have to try to understand how I got that way—whether it was perspiration, absorption, or genetics.

I like to think of myself as someone from whom you might learn something valuable, and someone to whom you might teach something valuable known to you. What should that be called? How about "Jerry" for me and "Dwayne" for you?

PHIL TRICE

Sometimes, I refer to someone as a "guru" with good intentions, but I usually feel put-on, manipulated, boxed-in, and maybe vaguely insulted if I'm called a guru. I like Jerry's suggestion; I was thinking that I prefer to be called Phil.

However, I do think there is some use to being able to talk about the state of one's fluency or depth in a field. In that regard, I keep thinking of Feynman using calculus differently than his students because he invented it himself. Of course, it had already been invented, and he already knew about it, but he sort of reinvented it himself. It seems that access to the invention of a field or tool may come along with some more freedoms or more subtle fluencies in its use. And just because somebody else already invented it is no reason not to do it again (for the first time).

Besides, I never liked the idea of getting stuck at the guru stage.

JERRY WEINBERG
Or at any stage!

Not Labeling, but Hypothesizing

BOB KING
Jerry's comments on labeling people have caused me to think about the times that I have been labeled and times that I have labeled others. Whether I like it or not, I believe that I classify or label people when I first meet them. And, when I introduce myself, I frequently do it by labeling myself somehow. In both cases, I think that this is a way for me to establish some foundation for beginning the interaction.

For me, there may be some advantage to labeling or classifying someone as a means to begin to understand them better. But I must be willing to let go of those labels when the other person becomes better known to me.

JERRY WEINBERG
I'd rather say that I "hypothesize" about people when I first meet them. That builds in the gathering of more information and the letting go of the hypothesis as the new picture builds up. At the same time, I definitely have a "bozo bit" on people. Once it gets set, it's not easy for new information to get into my picture.

Be an Expert Who Can Teach Expertness

DON GRAY
A guru is an expert with a following of groupies.

Jerry Weinberg
You mean "gurupies"?

Don Gray
Perhaps a portion of the old definition of a "consultant"—more than fifty miles from home—applies, too?

Jerry Weinberg
In medicine, they say that an expert is anyone who's more than fifty miles from home and does rectal examinations. That may or may not apply here.

Don Gray
Perhaps a difference between a guru and an expert could be that an expert can *do* the "expertness," where a guru can *teach* the "expertness."

Jerry Weinberg
That's an important difference, one that experts don't usually notice. A lot of experts believe they are teaching expertness, and don't realize they're only teaching expertise—at most.

Be Recognized by Other Gurus as a Guru

Steve Jackson
What about those at the highest levels—who grades them? I once asked my martial arts grandmaster who certified masters as masters. He told me that one knows when he's a master, and other masters will recognize him as such. I guess a guru knows he/she is a guru, and other gurus will recognize him/her also.

Jerry Weinberg
This reminds me of a client who came to me with an unusual problem: One of his programmers wanted to put the title "Guru" on his business card. I talked to the kid (he was 21) and asked him if he thought I was a guru. "Oh, yes," he told me, so I showed him my business card. Of course, it has no title on it.

Not calling myself a "guru" doesn't necessarily make me one, but calling myself one certainly disqualifies me. If I don't know that people will recognize me for what I am, then I can hardly be a guru.

Transcend the Realities Others Live In

Marianne Tromp
I like all these descriptions of the facets of a guru. Here is another one, I think. A guru is someone who can recognize the realities that others live in and how to transcend them. I'm trying to summarize something that I don't quite have words for, so let me describe a situation I've been in.

I used to live with a fellow who designed computers. When we would discuss technology, I understood what he was talking about. We had many good conversations and I agreed with his point of view.

But if I had a conversation with one of this fellow's coworkers, one-on-one, my friend's ideas were often discounted as being wrong somehow. In this conversation, I could follow the reasoning and agree with it.

I could never connect the different conversations. It was as though each person had different rules for their reality, and the two could not coexist for me. To me, a guru would be able to comprehend what differentiated the two individuals' worlds and transcend those differences. Perhaps that means a guru would be capable of translating one person's world into another's; or perhaps a guru could make each person aware of the limits of their own reality so they could communicate with each other.

George Olsen
I've found enough of the concepts in Jerry's books to be applicable to life outside work that I think it may be possible to recast things in terms that students might understand better because it relates to things they can observe in their own life. Relationships might be a good way of introducing some of Satir's ideas on communication. Dealing with change is another obvious hook for college students.

JERRY WEINBERG
The other day, I got a note from an editor who suggested that I "translate" some of my books into more general contexts than software engineering. I've had trouble with this idea because I don't feel I have sufficient examples from nontechnical businesses to "hook" readers from those areas. I think *Dilbert* captures this side of things better than I could (though the examples come from an organization that has been a client of mine for many years).

GEORGE OLSEN
I think that translating your books to different realities is a great idea. I've been trying to get other people interested in your work, but at least in the arts field, there's the "nerd factor" that needs to be overcome to convince people that software engineering relates to what they do.

I realize your work is more applicable to businesses that create intellectual properties (such as software, graphic design, or films) than to companies that make widgets. However, I think you might be surprised at how easy it would be to find similar examples from areas outside software engineering, if you work on talking to people in other fields. *Fast Company* magazine thinks along some of the same lines you do, so you might watch there for people in other fields to talk to.

Know the Difference Between the Map and the Territory

JERRY WEINBERG
The story goes that Picasso was once asked to explain his "Nude Descending a Staircase." He replied, "If I could have explained it, I wouldn't have painted it."

DANIEL STARR
He didn't paint it. The famous Cubist work "Nude Descending a Staircase" was painted by Marcel Duchamp. In any case, the painting is its own explanation; no further explanation is either necessary or possible. What do you see?

Jerry Weinberg

Now I'm in a complete funk. I don't know if I got the painting wrong or the painter wrong, or both. I guess that settles the question of whether or not I'm a guru.

So, let me try again, with a different story. I think it was Monet, or Manet, or Matisse, or somebody starting with *M*, who was told by a woman at an exhibition that one of his paintings didn't look like a woman. He replied, "It's not a woman; it's a picture of a woman." That is, we always have the question of whether someone's a guru or a picture of a guru.

Bill Trierweiler

There is a famous painting by Magritte of a pipe, with the following legend under the pipe:

Ceci n'est pas une pipe.

"This is not a pipe." I do not know if this is what you were thinking of.

Jerry Weinberg

Thanks for trying to bail me out. I suspect that "thinking" is too strong a word. I also suspect that a good line like this was used by many painters, even some whose names did not begin with *M*.

In the Swedish Army, they teach the recruits, "When the map and the territory don't agree, believe the territory." I think that as the semanticists say, the guru knows the difference between the map and the territory.

To bring this full circle, I recently heard the story of the businessman traveling in a train compartment with Picasso. When he realized who his companion was, he complained, "Why don't you paint real women? That's not what women look like."

Picasso asked him what real women looked like, and the businessman extracted a photo of his wife from his wallet, handing it to the artist. Picasso turned the photo over in his hands, then said, "So this is your wife? She's awfully small. And very thin." The guru knows the difference between the thing and the picture of the thing—which seldom makes other people happy.

Be Content to Be Content

Dwayne Phillips
Looking back, I realize that I attempted to be a guru about four years ago, and it did not work for me or anyone else. As I mentioned, I am the guru today in a different job (everyone calls me that, even though it irritates me). Today's guru experience seems to be working. Then, back four years ago, there was another guru on the job.

Why am I a better guru today, and why did this other guy succeed at being a guru four years ago?

Four years ago, I was trying *very* hard to get a pay raise. Today, I am not. Four years ago, the successful guru was not.

Contentment. I believe that is the answer. Accepting much about yourself, your position, your salary, your family, and deciding to be happy with the situation. I spent 1995 and 1996 in West Africa. When I returned to the affluent suburbs of Washington, D.C., I discovered that everything was acceptable and I was *very* happy to be there. I don't feel the great push to get a pay raise, impress people, move mountains, conquer the world, and so on.

People actually listen to me now. They even ask me for advice on topics I know nothing about. Contentment and happiness. I think there is something to those emotions.

Jerry Weinberg
The Buddhists speak of the contentment with being content—which is a feeling about the feeling. It sounds like Dwayne has it.

Be Accessible and Humble

Phil Fuhrer
To me, a guru has the attribute of being accessible. Some experts are gurus, but others put visible or invisible barriers

around themselves that make it clear that their expertise is for their own benefit and not yours. Gurus are also wise enough not to push their advice on others.

I guess we can add the category of "false guru"—someone who sits around and looks wise and accessible but does not have the expertise to give good advice or the wisdom to say "I can't help."

GEORGE OLSEN
Not sure where it fits in here, but it also struck me that humility is a factor, too.

Be Emotional

JERRY WEINBERG
So, although so far we've emphasized the intellectual qualities of a guru, what about emotional qualities?

PETE TERMAAT
Following are some of the emotional qualities a guru should have:

- *Patience.* No need to blurt out an answer to show off one's knowledge, or to rescue the student with a quick answer.
- *Gentleness.* The ability to nudge.
- *Playfulness.* Sometimes, the guru takes a stance such as "I know, but I'm not telling!" or "Let's explore!" This can seem snotty if it's not done well.
- *Enthusiasm* for learning, for discovery.
- *Empathy.* Compassion for beginners and confused people. In therapy, a guru needs the emotional agility to dart back and forth between feeling the client's emotions and keeping an outside perspective.

Sheldon Kopp's *If You Meet the Buddha on the Road, Kill Him!* begins with two chapters discussing disciples and gurus.[1] Most of what he writes has already been said in this thread.

[1] Sheldon B. Kopp, *If You Meet the Buddha on the Road, Kill Him!* (New York: Bantam Dell Publishing, 1982).

One thing Kopp emphasizes is that "the guru teaches indirectly, not by way of dogma and lecture, but by means of parable and metaphor."

Kopp uses a Sufi Teaching Story to argue that the truth, in the form of facts, does *not* set people free. The story sticks in my head and helps me be patient in situations where empathy is more powerful than advice.

Jerry Weinberg

Kopp's story relates the different reactions of two men entering the Land of Fools and being told that a watermelon was a monster. One killed the "monster" and ate some watermelon, which made the people think he was more of a monster himself. The other simply agreed that the melon might actually be a monster, then gained their confidence and spent a long time teaching them about melons.

It's a very nice example of change artistry. The second step is always making contact—after centering yourself so you don't have to show off how smart you are in the land of fools.

Lessons

JERRY WEINBERG

Labeling someone a guru can make him or her feel uncomfortable—even degraded. But if you insist on it, here are some characteristics of "a guru":

1. A guru is an expert with a following of groupies, or "gurupies."
2. A difference between a guru and an expert could be that an expert can *do* the "expert-ness," where a guru can *teach* the "expert-ness."
3. A guru knows he or she is a guru, and other gurus will recognize him or her, also.
4. Not calling myself "guru" doesn't necessarily make me a guru, but calling myself one certainly disqualifies me.
5. A guru is someone who can recognize the realities that others live in and how to transcend them.
6. We always have the question of whether someone's a guru or a picture of a guru.
7. A guru is content to be content.
8. A guru is accessible and humble.
9. And finally, a guru exhibits patience, gentleness, playfulness, enthusiasm for learning, and empathy.

7

The Leader as Learner

The Thread

How does the expert become an expert? How does the guru become a guru?

Inquiring minds want to know, so this chapter will extract those parts of our expert/guru thread in which Shapers talk about how they learned to be the experts they are.

—Jerry Weinberg

Learn at a High Level

STEVE JACKSON

I looked at some of my college notes for a course on the levels of learning. I think this applies to the question of what makes a guru. Following is a paraphrase:

- The first level of understanding is "awareness"—knowing the names of things and having some sense of what's good and what's bad.
- The second level is "literacy"—being able to compare and explain.
- The third level is "conceptual use"—being able to relate a concept to a specific use and to apply the material for issues, problems, and tasks in a given area.
- The fourth level is "application"—being able to apply material to a real-life situation.
- The fifth level is "skilled use"—this is rarely attained in an academic setting.

My opinion would be that a person could be considered a guru at levels 3 through 5, depending on who was doing the grading. Anyone at a lower level may consider anyone at a higher level to be a guru.

JERRY WEINBERG
There's a level zero, of course, which I put into my model of six software subcultural patterns. That level is "Oblivious."[1]

Be Both Inventive and Traditional

PAT FERDINANDI
I'm surprised to see that no one came up with inventiveness as a characteristic of gurus. When I think of those who I consider at the level of guru, I notice that they added something to the field to make it a bit better.

And yes, I agree that being able to teach (and write) your expertise to those at the lower levels of knowledge is an additional quality.

JERRY WEINBERG
Interesting. I don't know if inventiveness is part of the original meaning of "guru," which seems to me to carry a connotation of preserving the deep traditions of a deeply traditional society—which of course may not fit the style of a USA-twenty-first-century-high-tech type of guru.

PAT FERDINANDI
Inventiveness may not fit the twenty-first-century definition, either, but wouldn't it be nice if that were true or became true? People should always try to improve themselves as well as their profession. (Oops, my value system is coming through a bit strong . . . sorry!)

Immerse Yourself in a Virtuous Learning Cycle

BOB KING
A guru has established patterns in her life that make her feel alive and has abolished those patterns that have previously sucked life from her. She has found a positive feedback loop wherein her behaviors and experiences virtuously feed upon one another to continually add to her feeling of being alive. (My apologies to Christopher Alexander for this summation.)

[1] Gerald M. Weinberg, *Quality Software Management, Vol. 1: Systems Thinking* (New York: Dorset House Publishing, 1992), p. 23.

We learn from (and marvel in) gurus by being a part of the way they live their lives. In some cases, if not many, the positive feedback loop that gurus have created for themselves involves teaching. In those cases, gurus teach how to find the courage to establish one's own positive feedback loop and support its creation. They do not teach how to mimic the loop that they have created for themselves.

Is that different from an expert?

Yes. An expert has mastered a skill or body of knowledge to the point that she can perform that skill or use that body of knowledge better than many of her peers.

Have Personal Experience

George Olsen

For me, there are a couple of differences between being a guru and being an expert. To become a guru, being an expert is a prerequisite. This includes knowing the rules and knowing how and when to break them without having to think about it (in other words, unconscious competency).

But I also think there are several additional requirements. First among them is *personal experience in the related field of expertise.* Those who lack this personal experience may make great coaches—Bela Karolyi, for example, is a great coach without being a women's gymnast himself—but there will always be a certain something lacking. For example, a male doctor may be adept at helping women give birth and may have witnessed numerous women giving birth, but he'll always lack a certain insight possessed by a female doctor who has given birth herself.

This doesn't mean gurus have to know every detail in the field, however; merely enough that they're considered expert in it. Likewise, their knowledge could be stretched into related fields, as long as they know the point at which their personal experience ends.

Jerry Weinberg

I agree with this principle, and I think experience in the field can also be an impediment to would-be gurus—those who cannot get beyond their personal experience and see that mastery is a combination of the field and the individual. Thus, they are unable to offer different counsel to different individuals. They tend to say, "Just do it the way I did it."

Be Self-Aware

George Olsen
Another prerequisite to becoming a guru is *the ability to be aware of what you're doing.* I was tempted to call this "conscious competency," but that term has already been taken. "Self-aware competency" is a bit of a mouthful, but it does capture what I'm trying to convey.

I happen to be an expert in several graphics and HTML programs, so people come to me for advice. Unfortunately, I've learned the programs so well that although I know a particular shortcut, I sometimes can't say what key commands I use to do it (I am unconsciously competent). Fortunately, in this case, it's pretty easy to become self-aware—either I sit down at the keyboard and watch what my hands do, or I look it up in the manual.

Jerry Weinberg
Not for me. When I watch my hands, they don't do it.

George Olsen
Most things aren't this easy, particularly if they involve complex systems, such as graphic design, programming, or skiing. I'm going through this right now, writing an article about how to author Web pages that look the same across different browsers and different platforms. I've come to realize how much intuitive knowledge I've built up on this issue, and it's been fun trying to track down the specifics of why I "know" to do something one way and not another.

But there's more to "self-aware competency" than simply being self-aware: Your awareness needs to be accurate. For example, Cezanne was never a verbal guy and never really theorized about his art. However, since French artists of the period were expected to have theories, he ended up writing some down toward the end of his life. The problem is that his description of what he was doing contradicts what actually appears on the canvas. Consequently, art historians have generally disregarded his words and focused on the art, which arguably was the clearer expression of his ideas.

Don Gray
What's that Zen thing? If you describe it you don't know it?

I'm thinking of an old Chinese saying: "What I know fills me. What I do not know fills the universe."

What are the skies like where you live?

Be Able to Communicate Your Expertise

George Olsen
Another prerequisite to becoming a guru: Once experts have personal experience and self-aware competency, they need to *be able to communicate their expertise.* This is what really starts separating the gurus from the experts. This requirement probably includes a decent amount of competency in verbal skills, since true expertise not only involves knowing how to do something but why—and that's hard to communicate any way but verbally.

That's not to say other types of intelligence aren't useful. For example, teachers of Chinese brush painting will move the student's hand through the motions. Obviously, this method has more impact than merely telling the student how to do the stroke.

Another requirement is that the guru remember what it's like *not* to be competent. That's a major failing with many teachers who go through material before the students have really learned it, or who grow frustrated at the students' "lack of progress."

Jerry Weinberg
I sometimes get impatient like this because I'm confusing current students with earlier ones. "I taught you this thirty years ago. How come you still don't know it?" (This to a twenty-three-year-old student!)

Pat Ferdinandi
So many times, I have to remind myself that people may not have had the good fortune of being exposed to good practices—no matter what their age.

George Olsen
Yes, gurus need to be smart enough to realize which lessons can only be discovered by the students themselves. The guru may point the students in the right direction and nudge them as needed, but knows that discovering something yourself can have far more impact than being told about the same discovery. In a similar vein, gurus have to be able to admit the limits of their knowledge.

So far, we're still in the realm of "expert and good teacher," but the final difference is that a guru can teach expertness, not just expertise (as Jerry put it, earlier).

Jerry Weinberg
Teaching others both sharpens and tests your own knowledge. Ultimately, if you can't communicate with others, your own status as an expert is suspect.

Be a Guide to Spiritual Enlightenment

Steve Smith
My favorite definition of an expert is a person who can help someone turn a predicament into a problem that can be solved.

A guru is a person who has discovered spiritual enlightenment and can help guide someone else on his quest to discover his own spiritual enlightenment. To be an expert, an expert only has to help himself. To be a guru, a guru must help others.

For most people (including me), spiritual enlightenment is a predicament, so a guru must also be an expert.

Jerry Weinberg
I don't know if you have to have *achieved* "spiritual enlightenment" to teach others, but if you're not pursuing your own enlightenment, you're unlikely to enlighten anyone else.

Do Not Need to Be Omnipotent

Sue Petersen

A true guru can separate his or her issues from the student's issue. A true guru doesn't *need* to *help* a student. And, that emotional release frees the student to learn, or not to learn, whatever lessons the student needs to learn.

A true guru is not omnipotent, and doesn't *need* to be.

Remember That There Are Some Things Even a Guru Can't Do

Steve Jackson

I think that all of us need to be reminded from time to time that there are still some things that even gurus cannot do.

We don't need to beat ourselves up because there are some people we can't reach. Even God couldn't reach Satan (or so I'm told).

Jerry Weinberg

Thanks for the reminder, but are you sure you don't know about Satan from direct experience, you devil you?

Lessons

JERRY WEINBERG

Technical leadership and learning are inseparable, for many reasons:

1. Gurus teach others how to find the courage to establish their own positive feedback loop, and they support the creation of these feedback loops. They do not teach how to mimic the loop that they have created for themselves. Experts have mastered a skill or body of knowledge to the point that they can perform that skill or use that body of knowledge better than many of their peers.
2. Gurus have personal experience in their field of expertise, but they are able to get beyond their personal experience and see that mastery is a combination of the field and the individual.
3. Once gurus have personal experience and self-aware competency, they need to be able to communicate their expertise.
4. To be an expert, an expert only has to help himself. To be a guru, a guru must help others.
5. A true guru can separate his or her issues from the student's. A true guru doesn't need to help a student. And, that emotional release frees the student to learn, or not to learn, whatever lessons the student needs to learn.
6. A true guru is not omnipotent, and doesn't *need* to be.
7. There are some things that even gurus cannot do.

8

THE EXPERT AS TEACHER

The Thread

Earlier, George Olsen wrote: "Once gurus have personal experience and self-aware competency, then they need to *be able to communicate their expertise.* This is what really starts separating the gurus from the experts."

In this chapter, we'll look at what Shapers had to say about the expert as teacher.

—Jerry Weinberg

Provide More Choices

SUE PETERSEN

A guru is interested in giving his followers *more* choices. A true guru wants to make his followers *less* dependent on him.

An antiguru—an *urug,* in Jerry's terms—is chiefly interested in increasing his personal power and in feeding off the admiration and needs of others. An urug drains life and possibility from the world around him. A guru does the opposite; he adds energy, life, and empowerment to the universe.

GEORGE OLSEN

Sue's posting clarified something I couldn't quite express at the end of my last post.

True gurus are genuinely altruistic and interested in empowering their students. The humility I alluded to earlier is the gurus' lack of interest in using his or her power for self-aggrandizement and self-promotion.

Provide Distinctions

FREDRIC LAURENTINE

Guru is a word from India meaning "dark into light." The guru provides distinctions.

JERRY WEINBERG
Or, perhaps, provides an opportunity for others to see distinctions that they otherwise wouldn't see. Some people take the opportunity; some do not.

In any case, in order to provide choices, you have to provide distinctions. When we teach PSL, we often run two classes next door to each other. Within each class, we often have four teams, each working on the same problem. This parallelism is not intended to compare the students—to rank them or grade them. Instead, it gives the students a chance to see several ways to approach the same situation, each of which can be successful.

Let Them Experience Their Own Experience

BRETT SCHUCHERT
Some time ago, I experienced a realization (more like the realization experienced me, since it seemed to come from nowhere).

I had been teaching computer literacy courses since 1985 and had started working at my current company in 1993, teaching programming, analysis and design, and so forth. Eventually, I had written and taught our classes so many times that I had developed canned answers for every question—after teaching the same class more than thirty times, the new questions just didn't show up anymore.

One day, while I was teaching, I became aware that my answers were so refined they really didn't say anything! I noticed this while giving an answer, and I tried to change my approach midstream.

Soon after that, though, I realized I was burned out on teaching, for several reasons, and I simply stopped doing it. I changed from training to consulting.

A major mistake I was making while teaching was trying to show people how to do things given all the current wisdom. In doing so, I often robbed students of the experience of working through the logical sequence of learning.

During my break from teaching, I spent a lot of time reflecting on how I teach and how to present material in general. As a result, I have taken to heart several general principles, including just-in-time learning and leading students through the "old and wrong" ways of doing things before showing them new and better ways of doing things.

About two months ago, I experienced the realization that I was no longer burned out. Now I am excited to start teaching Java. I've been using it heavily this year and am certain that each time I teach our Java classes, I will learn several things! I am in no way a Java guru and teaching will not necessarily get me there, but it is one path I know that will accelerate my learning curve.

Provide a Discovery Trail

STEVE JACKSON

I was glad to see Brett's comments; they somewhat mirror my past experiences.

Several years ago, one of my teachers showed me a teaching technique we've since improved and named "The Discovery Trail." What we do now is map out how we want the student to get to the course objective. We then plan backward from that, placing problems in branching solution paths with inviting signs to sort of lead the student to take the obvious solution. Later, at the next problem along the path, the student isn't able to progress to the next solution because something in the previous solution prevents it. The student must backtrack, discover what the false assumptions were in the previous solutions, resolve the problems with the new information, and then go on.

In many cases, we are able to reproduce the same conditions and the same thinking that occurred during the "historic discovery" of the problem solution, and the students come away with a much better perspective on why things are the way they are (in other words, because they got that way).

James Burke used this technique in his famous PBS series, *Connections.* He showed how past thinking led to modern day solutions.

There is no experience like personal experience, and personal experience is non-transferable. (Dang it!)

Don't Confuse Beginners

Brian Richter

About two years ago or so, at work, I became a regular at the lunchtime bridge game. When I started, I knew very little about the game, but through watching the existing regulars play and reading a few books, I was able to pick it up. Some time after starting, I thought that my mother might find the game enjoyable and went with her to some bridge lessons.

Since I've been writing software for many years now, it's hard to remember all of the stages that I went through (although I'm sure I could recall them if I gave it some thought). But it's easy to remember the stages I went through in playing bridge, because it happened within such a short time frame. And, since Mom has been playing for a shorter time than I have, I recognize her various stages of expertise as being stages I went through myself not long ago.

In the bridge lessons we took, I can also see the difference between the first series of lessons, where we had a textbook to guide us, and the second series, which was more free-form in its content. At times, in the free-form lessons, the teacher would casually mention things that we hadn't learned yet, or worse, contradict other things he had told us. This was not actually wrong, since there are some "rules" that a beginner should follow but an expert should know when to break. But the beginners in the class were left very confused as to when they should or should not follow these rules.

Sometimes, I try to use these experiences as a sort of microcosm for the relative macrocosm of software, and draw on them when communicating at work with colleagues of differing levels of experience and expertise. George's comments about remembering what it's like not to be competent and

Brett's comments about the students having to experience working through certain things themselves seem to ring true in both the macro and micro realms (and probably all other fields that are capable of having "gurus").

Jerry Weinberg

I wonder, though, if gurus are really for beginners. Perhaps you have to reach a certain level of expertise before you can start benefitting from the teaching methods that (some) gurus use. I know that our workshops (such as PSL) don't "work" when we offer them to groups of college students who have no work experience. Is that just something wrong with our teaching methods (as Brian suggests), or is it something essential about the need for experience (as Steve suggests)? What do you think?

George Olsen

I tend to agree that beginners need teachers rather than gurus. In the large part, I think this is because the guru focuses more on meta-learning than on helping the student learn a specific task. To take an example from skiing: When I was a beginner, I was focused on trying to snow-plow correctly so I wouldn't sideswipe a tree.

Only later, when I'd mastered intermediate-level skiing, could I then begin focusing on learning how to learn to be a better skier. I didn't have to worry about killer trees, so I could switch my attention to sensing what my body was doing or not doing and analyzing the differences between when I was doing something right and when I wasn't. This is similar to Steve's students on "The Discovery Trail," where they're not just learning the subject matter, they're learning about how they learn to solve problems.

To put it into "Weinbergian" terms, beginners are focused on the product (a specific skill or bit of knowledge) rather than the process. And they're like organizations in that they can't start anticipating until they can steer. Actually, this phrasing happens to be more apt than Jerry might realize. For example, in skiing, until you can steer over a single mogul, you can't really plan a path through a mogul field. You may try, but what happens is that the bump throws you in an unexpected direction, and that in turn throws you off in *another* unanticipated direction, and so on.

In the case of Jerry's college students, I think one reason PSL doesn't "work" is that they don't have the experience to really understand what's being talked about. It's sort of like trying to teach someone to ski in the middle of summer, when the ski run is a grassy slope. Yeah, you may be able to impart some concepts, but it isn't really "real" to them.

Be Up-Front with Oversimplification

GEORGE OLSEN
The other issue that Brian has put his finger on is that beginners are trying to assimilate so much information that they often need clear rules to follow in order to avoid overload. For example, when I was learning to ski, I was taught that when carving parallel turns, you *always* put your weight on the outside ski. Later, when I was a better skier, I learned about the exceptions.

One way I've found to deal with this in my own teaching is to be up-front about such oversimplifications. (Say something like, "For the moment, do it this way." And if the student presses about the issue, I usually say, "There *are* some exceptions or more complexities, but when you've mastered doing it this way, you'll have the foundation you'll need to deal with them.")

JERRY WEINBERG
I find that to be true in writing, as well. It's one thing to break grammatical rules that you don't even know. Mastery allows you to break the same rules differently. Usually.

Select Students

MARIANNE TROMP
With respect to Jerry's experience that PSL (the Problem Solving Leadership Workshop) doesn't work for college students, I

wondered if the college students weren't as self-selecting as those who sign up for PSL. The decision to attend PSL is often based on knowing your work, isn't it, Jerry? If that is the case, PSL attendees have some goals that mesh well with the workshop approach. Those goals may depend on experience.

JERRY WEINBERG

Yes, I think the self-selection is a factor. Once in a while we have college-student-like trouble with someone in a regular PSL, and almost always it turns out they were "sent" by someone—or felt they were.

Also, in line with your other comment, college students do come out of a different reality than working people. Perhaps if I were a guru, I could transcend that reality gap. (Well, maybe I can, but not with PSL. And, besides, I don't much *like* working in that college reality.)

WAYNE STRIDER

A very important ingredient of guruness is having contact with persons who willingly have an "open channel" through which to receive the guru's gifts. Is a guru a guru without any students? Hmmm, I wonder.

JERRY WEINBERG

Perhaps making people climb a mountain to have access to learning is the guru's way to be sure they want to learn?

Perhaps gurus need marketing departments, just like the rest of us?

Personally, I hate to be the one who "selects" my students. I much prefer some form of self-selection, but from time to time I have to let someone know that I am unable to find an "open channel" through which to reach them. Then I'm forced to realize that I'm not the guru I was beginning to think I was.

Speaking of gurus, I saw a program on the tube the other day that claimed that Rajneesh's followers poisoned food in restaurants to keep their opponents from voting against them in an election. Coming up the mountain may be more difficult, but I think it's a better test than willingness to poison people.

Engage Each Learner

Stuart Scott

I was interested to learn that the PSL approach has been less effective with college students than with self-selected (and presumably somewhat experienced) working stiffs. I've never attended any of Jerry's workshops, but a few years ago I decided I thoroughly disliked the "stand up and tell 'em everything you know" style of training, and I decided to find another way. I read several of Jerry's books, as well as other sources, to try to read between the lines and learn how an effective experiential workshop might be constructed. Eventually, I came up with four main objectives, and I've used these a number of times to create learning environments. They are the following:

1. *To stimulate in each participant a lasting interest in the topic.* In other words, since you can't really learn very much in a day or three (compared with what you can learn in a lifetime), concentrate on setting people up to learn over a lifetime.
2. *To engage each participant in active learning experiences that provide practical experience with a range of relevant skills or techniques.* Although I frequently remember what I hear, I would say that I really only learn what I do.
3. *To identify and target the real-world needs of each participant (with respect to the general topic).* I decided that it usually doesn't make sense for me to try to figure out even before I meet someone exactly what that person needs to know to deal with the challenges he or she faces.
4. *To provide each participant with practical skills that can be applied immediately in a variety of project environments.* I often ask participants to identify some technique or insight or idea that came to them in the course of our activities, one that they will put to use immediately. I welcome small learnings just as much as large ones, in the belief that even a small usable learning is more than I ever took away from many of the classes I've attended.

I don't know how close these come to the meta-objectives of PSL, but assuming they're in the ballpark, I can see why they don't necessarily work well with college students. College students still have wide horizons, and it's pretty hard to stimulate in people of that age a lasting interest in one topic. After all, they're used to resisting the efforts of teachers to stimulate interest in the teacher's subject. As to the third objective, they may not yet recognize their real-world needs, or their needs may be quite dissimilar to those of a practicing professional. Finally, it's hard to give them practical skills they can use now, since they may not be engaged in much real work.

Perhaps I'm straying a bit off the guru topic here in my first SHAPE posting, but those of you who knew me a few years ago on the CompuServe DCI-CASE forum won't be a bit surprised.

JERRY WEINBERG

Well, Stuart, you're right. I'm not surprised. But, in this forum, if you stray too far from the topic, I intervene and create a new topic, and I don't think this is too far at all. I'm fascinated by how well you've abstracted the principles on which we build our workshops, and how closely related they are to guru-like behavior.

Underlying all these objectives is the deeper objective—to connect with the learners where they are, personally, now, here. When that occurs, learning must follow.

With college students, I've found that they tend to be all over the place from moment to moment, which makes it hard for me to pin them down to the "you, here, now" mode. Perhaps if I were a guru, I could do that.

Connect with the Learners Where They Are

STUART SCOTT

Jerry wrote, "*Underlying all these objectives is the deeper objective—to connect with the learner where they are, personally, now, here. When that occurs, learning must follow.*"

Thank you for saying it so succinctly. I guess I've often taken a rather indirect route to connecting with learners. I have responded several times to a request for conventional technical training with a curriculum that looks conventional on paper but actually provides me with an opportunity to talk with the learners about their real concerns and needs. At first, I felt a little sneaky doing this, but I learned soon enough that people don't complain afterward that I didn't cover the right material—just the opposite, in fact.

A while back, I slipped a half-day workshop on congruence into the tail-end of a course on analytical methods. I'd never addressed congruence with a group of programmers before, and I was nervous, but afterward they all said it was the best part of the course and that they wished we had done it at the beginning instead of the end. So, as time goes on, I'm becoming less surreptitious and more direct about my objectives.

Jerry Weinberg

You can generally accomplish the same thing without outright dishonesty. Just put something in your course outline or description saying "handling student concerns and questions." You can put just about anything you want under that title, because as long as the students are concerned about it, they won't complain.

George Olsen

Stuart's comments were extremely valuable in preparing me for a class I'm about to teach. I'm going to incorporate his idea about asking the students if they feel they've gotten a technique or insight they can take away from the course and use immediately—this will help me check and see if I need to make any mid-course corrections.

Jerry Weinberg

I like to do that, to be sure the course has now paid for itself. Once that happens, I feel freer to attempt less certain things.

By the way, notice how Stuart just taught *you* something that you're taking away from the course (that is, his comment) and using immediately.

Teach on a "Pay as You Go" Plan

Stuart Scott

I've found that some people feel they need to identify a really big insight that they can apply, and they feel apologetic when they can't think of one. To counteract this tendency, I do what I can to help people identify smaller, more attainable learnings of value, and to make sure they don't underestimate the value of these things. I haven't been as successful as I'd like at overcoming this problem—I often feel that participants have overlooked useful little ideas because they're so hungry for big, life-changing revelations—but I don't know if there's anything more I could do. I'd be interested to learn more about the experience of other Shapers.

I was curious to see if people followed through on these commitments, so I decided to follow up. Six months after completing a course designed to help some consultants become better analysts, I asked my students to place a dollar value on the single greatest benefit that had resulted from their participation in the course. I found that people typically hadn't followed through on their specific commitments, yet many were able to identify a significant, measurable single-greatest-benefit (thanks for the idea, Jerry).

Here are two of my favorites. One woman said she saved a client $20,000 with one programming change that resulted from her relentless use of one simple learning: the question, "Do you mean . . . ?" (Thanks again, Jerry.) A project manager estimated he reduced the cost of wasted meeting time on his project by about $50,000 after seeing himself behaving incongruently in a videotaped technical review.

This feedback has increased my confidence that we usually expect too much learning from a course, and we grossly undervalue the things people actually learn.

Jerry Weinberg

I try to deal with this on a "pay as you go" basis—to see if they can identify one thing that will make the course pay for itself at least once. For those to whom even this is too much of a type-stretch, I simply ask, "Are you convinced that you will have (or have had) some change of behavior that will pay for the time and cost of this course?"

Later, I can try to put on a specific value by using the "greatest single benefit" measure. This usually gives such a large return-on-investment that nothing more is needed to justify the training.

Brett Schuchert

Stuart wrote, *"I often feel that participants have overlooked useful little ideas because they're so hungry for big, life-changing revelations."*

I think that paying attention to the little ideas distinguishes someone as a guru (well, at least as an expert). Ultimately, I think taking a simple idea and understanding all of its ramifications is at the essence of understanding (and therefore, of being a guru or expert). I'll suggest two examples:

1. Einstein removed the assumption that time was constant. He then followed through on all the ramifications of that thought and came up with the special theory of relativity. His ability to derive the theory of relativity, mostly through thought experiments along with tests that would confirm his theory, showed a fundamental understanding of the physics surrounding relativity.
2. I've been working with object-oriented programming for about eight years. Over that time, I've reduced all the hype and buzzwords down to two: coupling and cohesion. All concepts and buzzwords can be related back to these two concepts. People who I consider to be especially good in this field can relate to and have often come to the same conclusion. All the other hype and mystery is scaffolding. It helps to map experiences from one reality to the next. Ultimately, as understanding "happens," the scaffolding is no longer necessary and in fact may get in the way.

The error a person can make when attaining this understanding is forgetting the steps followed to get there. This is a mistake I've been guilty of in both teaching and mentoring. If you can both understand the essence *and* appreciate the effort, then you're a guru.

Jerry Weinberg

Many would-be gurus dismiss small exceptions to their grand schemes as "unimportant." This is simply a cover for not understanding all the ramifications—it's a good test for pseudo-guruness. The Einstein example is a particularly good one because he made his mark by thoroughly examining some "tiny" exceptions to current physics that others dismissed as unimportant.

I agree with you about coupling and cohesion, ideas that come from general systems thinking. (Larry Constantine was my "grandson" in the systems course I taught at the old IBM Systems Research Institute, and these concepts were taken from my notes. Of course, they weren't original with me, either.) My general systems books are attempts to derive such ideas from first principles. Some system designers find them very useful, but many find that they explore too many "ramifications."

Provide the Questions, Not the Answers

Pete TerMaat

Earlier, George Olsen wrote, *"The guru may point the students in the right direction and nudge them as needed, but knows that discovering something yourself can have far more impact than being told about the same discovery."*

Short version: I agree!

Long version, or "How I discovered for myself what George just told us about": While I was a graduate student, I stumbled across a copy of *Teaching As a Subversive Activity.*[1] The book did two things for me.

---

[1] Neil Postman and Charles Weingartner, *Teaching As a Subversive Activity* (New York: Delacorte Press, 1969).

1. *It ruined me as a student.* Though I had done well at the game of absorbing material and spitting it back when tested, I suddenly despised it.
2. *It lit a fire under me as a teacher.* Once I began to see teaching as "helping people help themselves" instead of "filling people with knowledge," I was hooked.

I was a teaching assistant for a "Using the Macintosh" course. Most of the instructors saw themselves as answer dispensers. Most students expected this, and appeared startled when I responded to their questions not with answers, but with questions. They expected, "Press F3!" and instead got "What have you tried so far?" Or, "Hmmm. . . . Any ideas?" My focus was not "how to use Microsoft Word," but "how to approach unfamiliar software."

It felt like judo at times, dodging requests for answers while encouraging students to explore, experiment, and even "fail" now and then.

JERRY WEINBERG
I prefer the aikido analogy, because you don't hurt them—but more of that another time.

PETE TERMAAT
Much later, I learned that therapy can be an intense version of the same game. I now volunteer at a crisis counseling hotline, where I must dodge "tell me what to do" requests and help the caller develop his or her own solution. (Much as I'd like to scream, "Simple! Leave the jerk!")

Perhaps this is my answer to "What makes a guru?" An expert has answers; a guru has questions.

Any questions?

JERRY WEINBERG
When the writing is so clear, why would I have questions?

I really like this. It reminds me of what my wife and partner, Dani, always says about the difference between sociologists and anthropologists: A sociologist goes into a situation seeking answers; an anthropologist, questions. And Dani's a guru if I ever met one—and, of course, an anthropologist.

Pete's examples suggest another essential point. It's not just enough to have questions ready; you must also be able to resist the temptation to yield to your clients' emotional distress and to let them define the kind of help they "must have" (answers). You must be ready to have some students walk away in disgust, searching for someone who will give them (often wrong) answers (that they cannot use).

Have a Sense of Timing

Henry Knapp

Wonderful topic. I especially enjoyed Pete TerMaat's succinct description: *"An expert has answers; a guru has questions."*

This description reminded me of an old systems idea that I first encountered in a book by Peter Ouspensky, a Russian philosopher and follower of G.I. Gurdjieff. Gurdjieff stated that all events occur as results of the actions of three forces: active force, passive force, and neutralizing force—also called first force, second force, and third force.

The event of learning requires first force from the student (the desire to learn); second force from both the student and the material (resistance to learning, perhaps in the form of lack of information, difficulty of understanding the material, laziness, lack of prerequisite knowledge, and so on); and third force (what Jerry might call a "transforming idea," that enters the impasse when the student is stuck and loosens the logjam).

The first force has to come from the student: He or she has to want to learn something. The second force appears almost as soon as the first force appears: The student always must overcome some difficulty in order to truly learn (that is, the student must change his or her behavior). When learning is occurring, a third force enters from outside the impasse the student is experiencing and enables the student to overcome the difficulty and learn.

The first and second forces are changed: The student learns and the difficulty is overcome. The third force is unchanged: It enters, supplies a "twist of the wrist"—the smallest intervention that can transform the situation—and then goes its way.

Jerry Weinberg

Actually, it's a "twist of the wrist *at the right moment*" that does it. Most people have the most trouble with the timing, probably because they're too busy trying to "do the right twist or do the twist right" to notice the moment.

Henry Knapp

Of course, what I've said is an oversimplification. Events interact with events, and even as the guru is teaching, he or she may also be learning from the teaching situation. The guru may be having trouble learning something, and the teaching situation may enter his or her impasse as the third force, transform the impasse, and allow him or her to learn.

All this leads to one possible understanding of why the guru has questions rather than answers, and why the guru has to have a neutral attitude in his or her interactions with students, not depending on them to satisfy his or her needs.

For learning to occur, the student must want to learn, and want to learn *what the guru wants to teach.* For example, if the student wants to learn "how to use Microsoft Word," and the guru wants to teach "how to learn to use unfamiliar software," teacher and learner may reach an impasse. However, if the guru is able to intervene when the student is at an impasse, and help the student learn what he or she wants to learn *as well as* what the guru wants to teach, the student may learn more than he or she realized was possible to learn.

No learning would occur without the student's desire to learn, the obstacle (in the example case, Microsoft Word), and the outside influence of the guru. The guru's influence operates most efficiently when he or she is unattached (in the Buddhist sense) to the character of the result produced and provides the minimum intervention necessary to enable the student to achieve the immediate goal (in this case, for example, deleting a sentence).

The theory that all events result from three forces converging in space and time is often hard to verify, because we tend to be blind to the influence of the third force, but I think it's correct. I've been able to verify it in a number of instances in which it wasn't at first obvious that it was operating. In my opinion, gurus understand the theory intuitively and apply it to teaching, often with surprisingly beneficial results.

Help People Discover What They Already Know

GEORGE OLSEN

Earlier, Pete said he liked my observation that "*The guru may point the students in the right direction and nudge them as needed, but knows that discovering something yourself can have far more impact than being told about the same discovery.*"

I had no idea I was being so prophetic.

I don't know how many PSL attendees are familiar with Jerry's work beforehand, but I had read most of Jerry's books, as well as Naomi Karten's. So, it was especially striking to find myself discovering lessons that I "knew" already, but was experiencing—and learning—in a much more vivid and deeper way.

PETE TERMAAT

This thread has touched on issues such as learning by doing; the roles of discovery, exploration, and failure when learning; and teacher as motivator versus teacher as expert. For more on these themes, I recommend the *Engines for Education* site:

http://www.ils.nwu.edu/~e_for_e/

Lessons

JERRY WEINBERG
True leadership may well be defined by the teaching relationship between the leader and followers.

1. A very important ingredient of guruness is having contact with persons who willingly have an "open channel" through which to receive the guru's gifts.
2. A guru is able to connect with the learner where they are, personally, now, here.
3. A guru is interested in giving his followers more choices. A true guru wants to make his followers less dependent on him.
4. The guru provides distinctions. Or, perhaps, provides an opportunity for others to see distinctions that they otherwise wouldn't see.
5. Beginners need teachers rather than gurus. Taking a simple idea and understanding all of its ramifications is at the essence of understanding (and therefore of being an expert), and it's a good test for pseudo-guruness.
7. An expert has answers; a guru has questions.
8. If you can both understand the essence *and* appreciate the effort, then you're a guru.

9

The Courage to Teach in Any Direction

The Thread

Becoming a technical leader requires much knowledge and a strong character. If you're going to lead from a position in a hierarchical organization, you must have a special kind of understanding. You may know more about an issue than your "superiors," but if you lack courage, you'll just swallow your knowledge and nothing will happen. On the other hand, if all you possess is brash knowledge, you'll only hurt yourself by trying to teach upward.

The following contribution from Peter Harris is about this kind of courage, a necessary ingredient for shaping a better environment. I hope it gives courage to others, just as Peopleware *gave courage to Peter.*[1]

—Jerry Weinberg

Give Your Boss Some Credit

PETER HARRIS

Here is a true, happy story that revolves around the book *Peopleware* and some unusually brave and clear-thinking managers.

At the end of September, I started a new job as chief architect at a small company. I found the company during an intensive job search, and during my interviews there, coming from a company that placed me in a cube (in which cube I first read *Peopleware* and understood why I was feeling stupid and ineffective), I was impressed by the prevalence of offices and common space. Though the company was too far from my home for me to commute happily, I knew that the company offices were scheduled to move early the following year to a building much nearer to my home.

---

1 Tom DeMarco and Timothy Lister, *Peopleware: Productive Projects and Teams*, 2nd ed. (New York: Dorset House Publishing, 1999).

The morning of my second day on the job, a Wednesday, the head of the company sent around an e-mail describing his plan for the design of our new space—it was to be made up entirely of cubes! My jaw dropped; my heart raced; my telephone rang! I'd just come from that layout, and its lashes were still raw on my back. What to do! What to do? As a programmer of long standing, I did the only thing I could: I wrote a flame.

But I didn't send it. I felt better after writing it, enough to realize that I needed to do something more effective to protect my future comfort and sanity, and I needed to do it quickly, as the executive committee was to meet on Friday to approve a space plan. At about this point, the crystallization of my understanding of the situation came back to me: *Peopleware.* But my copy was out on loan to a colleague, then in Africa (yes, really).

I felt trapped. I needed to get a copy of it fast. Remember, I was new to this company (Could I take a long lunch?) and new to that area (Where are the bookstores?). Though my initial reactions were personal, my concern was also the happiness and productivity of the people I had signed on to guide. (I didn't want to work with and depend on the cube-otomied!) I decided that the most productive thing I could do that day was track down a copy of *Peopleware*, and I set out to find one.

Two hours later, at the fifth bookstore, I found a copy! Back at work, I wrote a short note suggesting to the CEO that he read Part II of the book before finalizing his plans for the new building. Then, I waited.

The following Monday, I, and everyone else, received the results of the discussions between the executive committee and the CEO. Lo and behold, the plan was completely different from the original cubes. We are building one- and two-person offices, with common areas sited throughout the building, for groups to gather informally. Each department has a hand in designing their own space. In short, our CEO read *Peopleware* and revised our layout along the lines suggested.

A week later, having bought his own copy, the CEO returned *Peopleware* to me with the words, "Thanks for lending me that. It's the best book on management I've ever read." He is the clearest-thinking CEO that I've ever had. Since it's such common sense, it must be very easy and terribly tempting to put aside the reasoning in *Peopleware.*

That's the story. We move in February. I've thanked Tom DeMarco and Tim Lister for writing *Peopleware.* Without it, I would have let the Furniture Police lock me up and throw away my brain. Flow deprivation—the short road to temporary psychosis.

DON GRAY

I have always made a point of giving books to people who impact my work. For client company programmers, this may be *Code Complete.*[2] For management, *The Fifth Discipline.*[3] Someone is going to suggest what to think. Why shouldn't it be me?

I'm not to the point yet where I can give away Jerry's *Quality Software Management* series,[4] but it is always recommended.

Balance Self-Worth and Safety

KEVIN HUIGENS

As I read about giving books to people to influence them, my initial reaction was to start listing reasons why that hasn't and wouldn't work for me here: Some people don't like to learn by reading; the ideas are usually met with the infamous "But Our Situation Is Different" argument; and so on. Fortunately, I was aware of my resistance (thanks to a SHAPE thread on paying attention to what's happening internally). So, I shifted my focus to my resistance.

---

2 Steve McConnell, *Code Complete: A Practical Handbook of Software Construction* (Redmond, Wash.: Microsoft Press, 1993).

3 Peter M. Senge, *The Fifth Discipline: The Art and Practice of the Learning Organization* (New York: Currency/Doubleday, 1994).

4 Gerald M. Weinberg, *Quality Software Management, Vol. 1: Systems Thinking* (New York: Dorset House Publishing, 1992); *Vol. 2: First-Order Measurement* (1993); *Vol. 3: Congruent Action* (1994); *Vol. 4: Anticipating Change* (1997).

My resistance only applies to those above me in the chain of command. I give my "subordinates" and my peers stuff to read, all the time. And I have in the past given articles and chapters to my "superiors" and that has sometimes been effective. So, my reaction to the idea surprises me.

What's the worst thing that could happen when I give my boss or his boss something to read? I'd be labeled as a malcontent troublemaker and somehow lose my job. What's the best thing? They could immediately implement the ideas in what I'd given them.

What's the most likely? They won't bother to read it.

What are some other possible outcomes? They'd read it and resist it, and I'd interpret the rejection of my ideas as a rejection of me, and that would lead to feelings of low self-worth. Or, they'd read it and feel bad about themselves, and then be angry at me for "making" them feel bad. (Yes, I know I don't really have that kind of power over others, and that this is a good example of placating.)

Thanks to something I read on the Learning Organization mailing list, I've learned to reframe resistance as part of a balancing loop from systems thinking. So, what am I trying to keep in balance when I resist sharing others' writings with my bosses? I think it's my feelings of self-worth and safety. And my illusion that I can always change other people's thinking, that I'm "perfectly influential." Despite all of this, I will still continue to give my bosses things to read that I feel would be helpful.

Jerry Weinberg
I find it's easier to take such risks when I have money in the savings account. In this way, lots of my personal depression-baby fears can be rendered inoperative.

Luck Is Always a Factor (Especially If You Help)

Phil Fuhrer
I think Peter's note is about many things, and courage is not primary. Peter helped his new company rediscover one of the

important things that should not be changed. He did this in several remarkable ways.

In my experience, people are not fired for sending books. So, I think Peter found a relatively safe method of introducing the foreign element that prompted the rediscovery. Rather than risking himself by flaming and adding chaos, he took the risk that his transforming idea would not be heard.

Managers often ignore books by not reading them, or by missing the point. Managers have hundreds of books to read. It is remarkable that *Peopleware* was the right book for the right manager at the right time. Peter's manager must have been ready for rediscovery and change. The office rearrangement must have caused some chaos.

I am glad this all worked out so well, and we should not discount that luck is also a factor.

Jerry Weinberg
Yes, luck is always there, but I think Peter's astute (albeit intuitive) observation of people had even more to do with it. And, his timing. Also, you increase your chances of winning the lottery if you buy a ticket.

Don't Confuse Courageous with Dumb

Jim Jarrett
I just got back after two weeks of vacation over the holidays, and my cubicle environment exacerbated my reentry by a couple orders of magnitude.

On a first day back, I usually reenter gently by processing e-mail messages, voice mail, and other paperwork that has piled up and making a to-do list for the week. I also reconnect with friends and colleagues, letting the environment re-infuse me, and making my renewed presence known. I don't expect to get any "real work" done, and I try not to deal with any issue directly—I just add it to my list.

Yesterday, though, in my sad little cubicle, my reentry was shattered almost immediately: Within an hour, two nagging issues (or, rather, the bearers thereof) plunked themselves down in my cube, despite the open closet door I use as a makeshift office door to block the entrance. Unfortunately, the folks involved usually cannot be chased off with words—a locked barrier is usually required, and always unavailable. So, I had to deal with the "crises" and pull myself out of the warm and comfy vacation-mode I was in.

JERRY WEINBERG

The first thing that caught my eye was Jim's phrase, "Unfortunately, the folks involved usually cannot be chased off. . . ." If you put that in the active voice, it reads, "Unfortunately, I'm usually unable to chase off the folks involved. . . ." Perhaps you can learn about other ways of chasing than with words—how about a picture or sign to hold up? How about a dirty look? A clean look? Or try an aikido approach: Since you're just back from vacation, try inviting them in to see your extensive collection of vacation pictures.

JIM JARRETT

In the early afternoon, I realized that I had a mind-numbing headache. Beyond the stress of the morning, I believe it had a great deal to do with the bright and evil florescent lighting that beams down on me from the ceiling. This lighting has controls that are shared by twenty-three other cubes, so I can't just turn it off.

JERRY WEINBERG

Why not? Are you beginning to see your placating pattern? That usually produces headaches for me when I fall into it.

JIM JARRETT

Needless to say, I finished my workday less motivated, with less accomplished, and quite exhausted and grumpy.

JERRY WEINBERG

So much for empowerment!

JIM JARRETT

As for courage to change the environment, I've decided that this is one battle I don't have the energy to win. We moved into this brand new facility only eighteen months ago, and the Furniture Police were not really listening when they asked for feedback prior to the construction of the building. If you happen to be a manager here with at least twelve reports, you get an office (on the interior of the building). If you are director or higher, you can get a window. It's a gorgeous facility that the company constantly brags about, yet there are policies against the permanent booking of "project war-rooms" and tailoring any of the space for a specific department.

I'll express my courage in fighting for change on other issues, such as making quality software development a shared value among management; calling for explicit project transition planning (that takes into account the humans involved), as the huge, monolithic project I'm working on comes to a close; and building strong, productive teams that respect each other and grow together.

JERRY WEINBERG

Sounds like a smart approach, and it's easy to confuse courageous with dumb. Choosing your battlegrounds is an important part of a winning strategy. Nevertheless, if the lights are truly making you sick, I think that's a battle you can, and should, win. If necessary, you could contact (or threaten to contact) OSHA—and I know, as a long-time OSHA inspector in Verseworks. (That's a PSL in-joke, for those who don't know.)

Is What You're Getting Worth What You're Paying?

BRIAN RICHTER

The story about "chasing off" cubicle intruders reminded me of an environmental problem that I once had. On two different projects, there was someone who was giving me technical help with some of the mathematical aspects of what I was doing. When I needed his help, it was great to have him around, but he would often come around when I didn't need any help, usually when I was in the middle of something and didn't want to be disturbed. I did not want to alienate him, but I didn't want him interrupting me several times a day, either.

He also seemed to be one of those people who either couldn't or didn't want to pick up on subtle hints. Some people will readily take the hint that they're interrupting something (in fact, if I appear busy, most people ask, "Am I interrupting anything?" before they just start talking), but not my technical friend.

On the first of the two projects, it happened that some of the work was being done in a locked area, so I just moved into that area to run away from the interruptions.

On the second project, it wasn't so easy. I mentioned the problem to the project manager, but this approach didn't help. I found the situation difficult because my technical friend was quite a bit older than me, and I felt that he would easily get offended if I raised the issue with him.

JERRY WEINBERG
Yes, we old guys are pretty sensitive, so be sure you do whatever we want!

BRIAN RICHTER
If he got offended, he might not come around anymore, and I might not get the technical help I needed. The situation never really got resolved, and I ended up just putting up with his interruptions until the project was over.

JERRY WEINBERG
I don't think this is such a bad resolution. The interruptions were a price you paid for the advice, and you evidently thought it was worth it. If you hadn't, I think you could have found a way to help him regulate his interruptions. We old guys aren't really that sensitive, but we do sometimes get lonely.

Plant a Seed; Cultivate; Be Patient

MARK PASSOLT
In some cases, as in Peter Harris's situation, the window of opportunity for change is brief. However, in many cases, the

change we want to effect is to a long-standing practice, and if it takes time to evoke the change, that's okay.

My boss's practice has been not to hire people who only have a bachelor's degree. Almost all of our hiring is of new grad-school graduates. For the past two years, we've been under considerable pressure to increase our staffing, but since we're fussy about who we hire, we haven't met our targets. Even so, my boss was unwilling to consider B.S. grads. My observation and conviction were that we were missing some excellent engineers. What to do?

1. *Plant the seed.* Another manager and I routinely told our boss we were missing good candidates by not considering B.S. graduates. The communication was clear—he knew our thoughts and we knew his.
2. *Take action.* Action is a great way to start change. (And if you initiate the action, you have a better chance of guiding the change.) I discussed the idea with our marketing manager—he was tired of hearing that we didn't have enough staff to add all the features our customers wanted. I made it a point to interview B.S. students when I did on-campus recruiting. (My boss would probably have considered it a waste of time, had I made a point of telling him.) I got faculty members to recommend the best senior computer science students, and I brought one in for an interview. I sponsored a senior project for a team of four students.

The results: The project team gave a presentation to us in early January. My boss was impressed by the quality of their work and their maturity. He wants to hire at least one. And I haven't yet asked the professor if they are at the top of the class—he may recommend some who are even better!

Jerry Weinberg

Watch out, Mark! The top ones in the professor's academic view are not necessarily the ones you want to hire.

Mark Passolt
This change effort wasn't really all that big: My boss didn't have to change his values; we will still be plenty fussy about who we hire. However, I believe it will have a big impact on our organization.

Do I dare try to change this place? If I don't, I'm not doing my job.

Jerry Weinberg
So, when contemplating a change effort, you must first think about the *time scale*. The strategies and chances of success are quite different for the quick-fix and the long-term adaptation. Just as in writing code, trying to go too fast is the sure way to slow things down—or guarantee their failure.

Of course, it's possible to go so slow that nothing ever happens, but my experience says that situations are seldom the emergency that people make them out to be. Making everything an emergency is often a tactic for being sure that nothing ever changes. Most of Mark's change artistry would be useless if he were trying to influence a hiring decision that was taking place this week.

See Them As Human Beings

Henry Knapp
I've also had trouble getting bosses to adopt ideas that I think are helpful. I've just started trying to deal with my boss, my peers, and my subordinates as customers for my ideas. I haven't gotten very far with the idea yet, but I can already see that viewing people as customers evokes different feelings toward them than viewing them as bosses, peers, and subordinates, and I'm better able to avoid conditioned responses based on the "boss," "peer," and "subordinate" labels.

Jerry Weinberg
Thanks, Henry, for reminding me of the only thing I didn't like about *Peopleware*—namely, the title. For many years before the book came out, I had fought with people like Tom Gilb to stop using this term, which implied treating people like things.

Alas, the book came out and rooted this dehumanizing term into the computing lexicon. It seems to me that such a title—like the titles "boss" and "subordinate"—creates an incongruent communication before you ever get started. One of my principles is, "Don't bother to try communicating with any boss who insists on reminding you who's 'boss.'"

Lessons

Jerry Weinberg
Teaching individuals and organizations often involves counter-intuitive actions.

1. Courage is the willingness to "take risks on your own behalf," one of Virginia Satir's Five Freedoms.[5]
2. You increase your chances of winning the lottery if you buy a ticket.
3. It's easy to confuse courageous with dumb. Choosing your battlegrounds is an important part of a winning strategy.
4. When contemplating a change effort, you must first think about the time scale. The strategies used and the chances of success are quite different for the quick fix and the long-term adaptation.

[5] For more on the Five Freedoms, see Virginia Satir, *Making Contact* (Berkeley, Calif.: Celestial Arts, 1976).

10

The Courage to Be Yourself

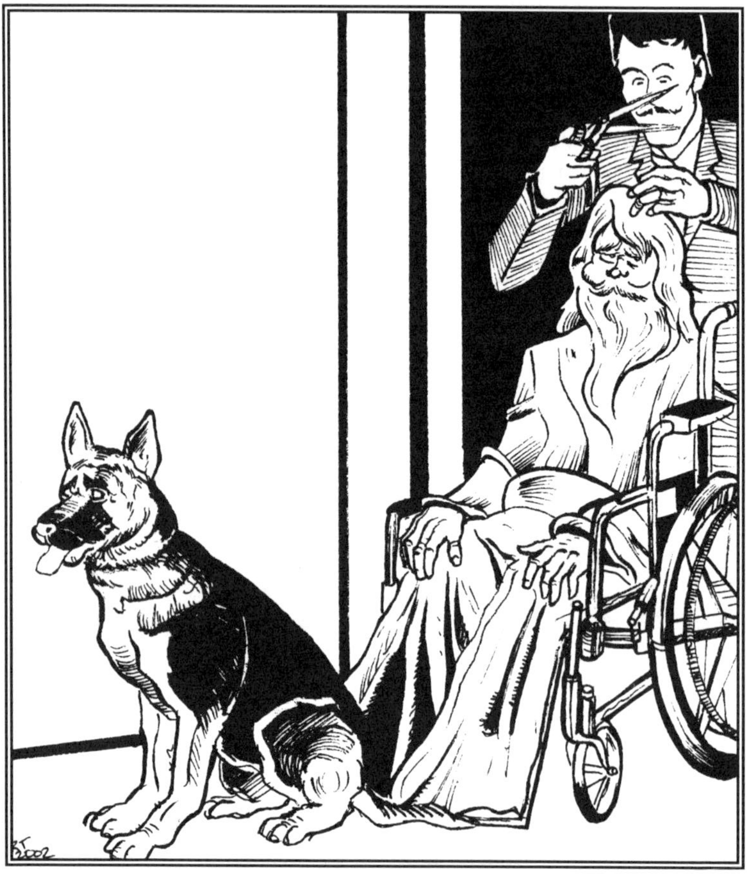

The Thread

Here's a note about job hunting from a member of one of my Software Engineering Management groups:

> *I've been on a major interview almost every day for the last few weeks, and I find that exhausting. I have been learning a lot about myself and where I want to head, though.*
>
> *Unlike last year, and the last job change, this time I haven't cut my hair. In fact, not cutting my hair has become as much of a symbol for me as cutting it was last time. It's simpler to represent myself to people as I am, rather than how I think they want me to be.*

As a consultant, I'm always looking for new jobs. As a bearded old guy, I've often wondered about shaving my beard in order to increase my chances; as a slob, I've wondered about changing the way I dress. I've written about dressing for the job, especially in The Secrets of Consulting, *and this correspondent's experience was instructive (and confirming) for me.*

To get his previous job, he cut his beautiful long hair. After only a few months, the company got in trouble and had to downsize. Its managers used the curious principle of classifying people on their "work fit" and their "culture fit." He was in the highest category on work, but in spite of cutting his hair, lowest on culture. Evidently, he hadn't fooled anybody.

They cut all the low scorers on culture, using the argument that they could teach people skills but

(CONTINUED)

(THE THREAD, CONTINUED)

couldn't change their culture. This was especially curious because he had been brought in as a specialist in culture change—precisely to change their culture.

We can draw several morals from this case:

1. *When applying for a job, don't bother trying to fool people about your true nature. Pretty soon the honeymoon period will be over, and they will see the truth. (This applies to marriage, as well.) In other words, the truth is not only simpler, it's more effective.*
2. *Worse than that, you will see the truth. If you have to change your true self to get the job, you don't belong there. My correspondent wasn't happy in the job, and his only regret is that they fired him before he took the initiative to quit.*
3. *Although you can't change your true nature for long (and live with yourself), you can learn. In this case, you can learn that lying (with words or actions) is never a good basis for starting a relationship you hope will last.*

Our question for this thread is: How do you decide how to present yourself to your employers and/or clients? How many steps do you take in their direction before you decide you've moved far enough?

—Jerry Weinberg

Don't Try to Be a Generation Younger

KAY WISE

When I started my MIS career, I was nearly a generation older than most of my coworkers. One morning before work, I put on my blue jeans, thinking I would fit in a little better with the crowd. Ken, my husband, looked disapprovingly at my attire, saying something like, "You're not really going to work looking like that, are you?" I changed back into my suit and have gone to work looking more or less "dressed up" ever since.

My seven years at that company were successful. I was well liked and well compensated. But I was never part of the programmer crowd. Before long, I was moved from product development over to the finance department. Three jobs later, I'm still dressing like an accountant and still working in finance.

Sometimes I wish I were a quick-thinking, fast-acting, fix-anything kind of coder, comfortable in blue jeans; sometimes I wish I were a smooth-talking salesman who stood out in a crowd; sometimes I wish I were a free-spirited artist, wearing colorful, creative combinations. But by dressing at work like the people I admire most, such people have helped me find my place in a culture where I am as comfortable with my team as I am with my clothes.

Here's the rest of the story. My Myers-Briggs type is INTP, with the emphasis on iNtuitive and Perceptive.[1] Most accountants are ISTJs with the emphasis on Sensing and Judging. Our strengths are highly complementary. We may be "birds of a feather," but we are not alike.

JERRY WEINBERG

Quite true, so it takes work to achieve the power of that complementarity, which you can do only if you communicate with one another.

---

[1] The Myers-Briggs Type Indicator (MBTI) is a system of classifying preferences in interaction, understanding, and decision-making style. It was developed by Katherine Cook Briggs and her daughter Isabell Myers-Briggs in the late 1920's and early 1930's. For more on MBTI, see Gerald M. Weinberg, *Quality Software Management, Vol. 3: Congruent Action* (New York: Dorset House Publishing, 1994).

Dress to Make Both of You Comfortable

Phil Fuhrer

Although I have a beard, my personal style is vanilla enough that I don't think I would have much difficulty adapting to a work environment where beards are unacceptable.

When I started reviewing projects, I wore a tie and dressed a little more formally than the people working on projects I reviewed. I found that this caused some subtle difficulties. The project members noticed my *outsided-ness* more and occasionally their managers would try to get me to assist them in "controlling" their staff. Now I try to dress like the people that I work with and err on the side of personal comfort.

By and Large, They'll Have to Resolve Their Own Chaos

Phil Fuhrer

I also have a story about one of my colleagues who dresses very casually. One time, he wore his typical biker-style jeans and T-shirt to a meeting we had with some architecture consultants in Houston. First, when the receptionist was logging us into the building, she gave him the express delivery packages instead of a building pass. Then, during the sessions, the chaos was obvious. The consultants couldn't determine whether he was a low-level observer learning our trade, an equal colleague with unusual style, or a high-powered person who could flaunt the dress codes. Of course, the answer was all three, and he did a good job of keeping them on the hook and letting them resolve their own chaos.

Daniel Starr

I am the person Phil Fuhrer was talking about, the biker-looking guy who put the high-powered architectural consultants into chaos. Even though the consultants were holding a paper that I'd written, they addressed their questions to my boss. He'd promptly hand each question off to me, I'd answer it, and then the consultants would ask their next question—

again, addressing my boss. This went on for an hour or so before they finally realized that the "biker" sitting at the conference table and the author of the paper had the same name, and maybe it *wasn't* just a coincidence.

Incidentally, we can laugh about this now, in part because once we got past the chaos induced by my appearance, we got quite a lot of productive work done. The consultants didn't appear to be bigoted, just confused!

JERRY WEINBERG

I learned this lesson from working with people in wheelchairs (for Paws With a Cause[2]). When you're in a wheelchair, people look at you differently. Some are confused, some are pitying, some are empathizing, and some (usually little kids) are delighted to see something new and interesting—especially if there's a dog pulling your chair!

So, there's more than one interpretation to people's reaction to the way you look. You don't get to change the reaction, but you get to change your interpretation. It may be harder at first, but in the long run, it's better to change your insides than to change your appearance. And the same goes for them.

If It's Not a Good Fit, Don't Do It

KEVIN HUIGENS

This thread relates to a problem I faced a few years ago. Through a headhunter, I interviewed here in Chicago for a position in the development center of a tire company. According to the recruiter, the manager really liked me and wanted me to come back for a second interview.

The catch was that I would have to shave off my beard and mustache because the company had a no-facial-hair policy. I turned down the offer. The recruiting firm hounded me for several days. The recruiters could not accept that they were going to lose out on a commission because of some whiskers.

---

[2] Jerry and Dani are field trainers for Paws With a Cause, an organization that furnishes trained service dogs for people in wheelchairs, people with hearing problems, and people who have seizures.

Jerry Weinberg
Could they accept that they were going to lose a commission because of some stupid company policy?

Kevin Huigens
Normally, I have problems expressing anger, but not in this case. They couldn't understand my reasoning that if the company had this silly policy, I anticipated that they had a lot more policies with which I would not agree.

Six months later, the tire company closed their development shop here and moved everything back to Ohio. Saved by my whiskers.

A year after that, I got another call from the same recruiters. The manager of the tire company's development center was now running a development center for a large food corporation. He was staffing up to roll out a CASE tool throughout the entire corporation in six months. He remembered me and wanted me for his staff. I was flattered but thought it a fool's errand. Again, the recruiters had trouble taking no for an answer. Six months later, the guy was still trying to hire staff to roll out the CASE tool.

Now it's getting time for me to move on from my current position. Not only do I still have my beard and mustache, but I've added a ponytail. (I look nothing like the ISTJ that I am.) I've also gotten used to nearly six years with a business casual (no tie) dress code. I don't own a suit anymore and don't really want to buy one. All of this is going to make my job hunt harder. Recruiting agencies aren't interested in me because I'm management, not technical, and because I won't play the game and do whatever it takes to get a job offer.

Jerry Weinberg
I think it's going to make your job hunting easier, unless you don't care what kind of job you get.

Kevin Huigens
I think you're right, Jerry, about telling the truth about one's nature. My goal in an interview is to determine if there would be a good fit between me and the company. That requires hon-

esty from both parties. The downside is this limits my options. At some point, I may need to rethink my requirements.

Adapt in Order to Communicate

SUE PETERSEN
I often find myself changing my presentation in an attempt to influence the person(s) I am communicating with. (Whether it's how I frame a logical argument or how I dress and carry myself.) For instance, I'm a high S (Sensing). I have a lot of N (iNtuitive) friends. I often find they don't understand me unless I can frame my message in a more "intuitive" fashion.

I wonder how this relates to the "shave the beard" story. I believe there are good ways to change myself, and bad ways. The extremes are easy to identify, but what about the murky stuff in the middle?

JERRY WEINBERG
There's no easy way to know if you've given too much, or taken too much. Every story has to be worked out on its own merits, as each of these stories shows.

Is It the Hair, or Is It the Arrogance?

DANIEL STARR
At the very beginning of my career, in an attempt to hold onto a job that I was in the process of losing, I got my hair cut back pretty radically (to something called "longer" hair—which is, of course, shorter than long hair). It didn't work. A few weeks later I was shown the door, shortened hair and all.

Cutting my hair hadn't saved my job, because growing it wasn't what got me in trouble, regardless of how it looked at the time. I had been somewhat ahead of schedule on a project that was somewhat behind schedule overall, and I figured this was because I was smarter than most of the people I was working with. I was, at times (all the time?), rather nasty about it. In short, I was in trouble not because I was a *long-haired* snot, but because I was a long-haired *snot*.

JERRY WEINBERG
This isn't exactly an original story. Consider that Bible story about cutting long hair. Samson was "cut down to size" not because they didn't like his hairstyle, but because he was too strong for them. I don't know if he was snotty about it, but as I recall the story, he was rather arrogant about his strength. The haircut taught him a lesson—as it seems to have done for you.

Who You Are Is More Important Than What You Wear

DANIEL STARR
In between jobs, a time I used to visit both coasts on my new motorcycle, I gave a lot of thought to how I might avoid repeating this experience. I realized that looking a little different was a part of who I am, so no haircuts for the next job. Next, I realized that I probably was smarter, or at least more effective, than most of the people I worked with. There didn't seem to be much I could do about that.

JERRY WEINBERG
There's that Samson bit again.

DANIEL STARR
This left the matter of my nasty attitude toward others. I have come to realize over time that it was a coping mechanism—the corporation demanded infinite work, and I didn't know any congruent ways to limit my load. So, I became something of a snot, using a nasty attitude and some highly-visible goofing off to make the point that I did as much work as anybody else but spent a lot less effort doing it.

I didn't really understand all that at the time; I just knew that I didn't like the person I sometimes appeared to be. So, in my subsequent jobs, I've kept my hair, continued to dress casually, and come to accept that I can do more work than a lot of other people. These are parts of who I am. And I've learned some more congruent, or at least quieter, ways to say no and control my load.

Lessons

JERRY WEINBERG

Often working as outsiders, we consultants may be tempted to change our personal style to fit in and get more jobs. Here are some suggestions for staying who you are, even when you have to convince people to hire you.

1. Don't fake it when applying for a job. You won't be able to keep it up, and neither will they.
2. In the absence of any better reason for dressing or acting in a certain way, you might as well be comfortable—for both of you.
3. Dressing might change your influence, but the relationship between dress and influence may not be as simple as you first think.
4. It's better to change your insides than to change your appearance.
5. The expression on your face is a lot more important than the hair on your face.

Bibliography

DeMarco, Tom, and Timothy Lister. *Peopleware: Productive Projects and Teams,* 2nd ed. New York: Dorset House Publishing, 1999.

Garfinkel, S.L., D. Wise, and S. Strassman. *The Unix Hater's Handbook.* New York: IDG Books, 1994.

Kopp, Sheldon B. *If You Meet the Buddha on the Road, Kill Him!* New York: Bantam Dell Publishing, 1982.

McConnell, Steve. *Code Complete: A Practical Handbook of Software Construction.* Redmond, Wash.: Microsoft Press, 1993.

Postman, Neil, and Charles Weingartner. *Teaching As a Subversive Activity.* New York: Delacorte Press, 1969.

Satir, Virginia. *Making Contact.* Berkeley, Calif.: Celestial Arts, 1976.

Senge, Peter M. *The Fifth Discipline: The Art and Practice of the Learning Organization.* New York: Currency/Doubleday, 1994.

Weinberg, Gerald M. *Becoming a Technical Leader: An Organic Problem-Solving Approach.* New York: Dorset House Publishing, 1986.

———. *Quality Software Management, Vol. 1: Systems Thinking.* New York: Dorset House Publishing, 1992.

———. *Quality Software Management, Vol. 2: First-Order Measurement.* New York: Dorset House Publishing, 1993.

———. *Quality Software Management, Vol. 3: Congruent Action.* New York: Dorset House Publishing, 1994.

———. *Quality Software Management, Vol. 4: Anticipating Change.* New York: Dorset House Publishing, 1997.

———. *The Secrets of Consulting: A Guide to Giving and Getting Advice Successfully.* New York: Dorset House Publishing, 1985.

INDEX

BIN TRAVERLER FORM

Cut By: Georgette Isturiz # Qty 26 Date 10-07-26

Scanned By: ____________ Qty ______ Date ____________

Scanned Batch ID's

____________ ____________ ____________

Notes / Exceptions

____